THE ART OF

UZBEK COOKING

Hippocrene is NUMBER ONE in
International Cookbooks

Africa and Oceania
Best of Regional African Cooking
Egyptian Cooking
Good Food from Australia
Traditional South African
  Cookery

Asia and Near East
Best of Goan Cooking
Best of Kashmiri Cooking
The Joy of Chinese Cooking
The Art of South Indian
  Cooking
The Art of Persian Cooking
The Art of Israeli Cooking
The Art of Turkish Cooking

Mediterranean
Best of Greek Cuisine
Taste of Malta
A Spanish Family Cookbook

Western Europe
Art of Dutch Cooking
Best of Austrian Cuisine
A Belgian Cookbook
Celtic Cookbook
English Royal Cookbook
The Swiss Cookbook
Traditional Recipes from Old
  England
The Art of Irish Cooking
Traditional Food from Scotland
Traditional Food from Wales

Scandinavia
Best of Scandinavian Cooking
The Best of Finnish Cooking
The Best of Smorgasbord
  Cooking
Good Food from Sweden

Central Europe
Best of Albanian Cooking
All Along the Danube
Bavarian Cooking
Traditional Bulgarian Cooking
The Best of Czech Cooking
The Art of Hungarian Cooking
Lithuanian Cooking
Polish Heritage Cookery
The Best of Polish Cooking
Old Warsaw Cookbook
Old Polish Traditions
Taste of Romania

Eastern Europe
The Cuisine of Armenia
The Best of Russian Cooking
The Best of Ukrainian Cuisine

Americas
Cooking the Caribbean Way
Mayan Cooking
The Honey Cookbook
The Art of Brazilian Cookery
The Art of South American
  Cookery

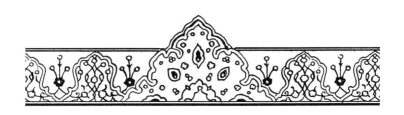

THE ART OF

UZBEK COOKING

LYNN VISSON

HIPPOCRENE BOOKS, INC.
New York

ISBN 0-7818-0669-0

For information, address:
HIPPOCRENE BOOKS, INC.
171 Madison Avenue
New York, NY 10016

Printed in the United States of America

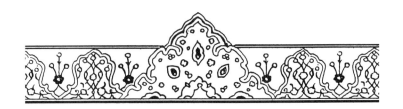

TABLE OF CONTENTS

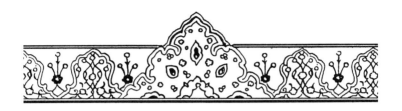

INTRODUCTION

Silks and spices, gold and Genghis Khan, Tamerlane and Tashkent, minarets and markets—today's Republic of Uzbekistan is a blend of exotic peoples and places, a historical crossroads of the trade winds and intellectual currents which swept across Asia and Europe for centuries. For decades caravans traveling along the Silk Route stopped to gape in awe at the blazing blue domes of Samarkand and the white mosques and minarets of Bukhara.

A country with an area slightly larger than that of California, Uzbekistan has a geographic terrain which runs the gamut from huge flat plains to soaring peaks. To the north of the country is the Aral Sea; to the northwest lies the Kizyl-Kum (Red Sands) desert and its oases, while the mountain ranges of Tien-Shan and the Pamir valley run to the south and east. About three fifths of the land is desert steppe, dotted with fertile, irrigated oases along the banks of the two large rivers, the Amu Darya and the Syr Darya. Broad pastures and mountain streams are home to the sheep who produce the country's rich supply of lamb. The fertile soil yields a rich harvest of fruit, vegetables and cotton; Uzbekistan is the world's fourth largest cotton producer. The hot, dry summers which last from May to September and the water for irrigation create excellent conditions for growing cotton, fruit and vegetables.

A neighbor of the four other Central Asian countries of Kazakhstan, Turkmenistan, Kyrgyzstan and Tajikistan, Uzbekistan also borders on Afghanistan. The 23 million people who live in Uzbekistan represent a wide variety of nationalities, for while Uzbeks account for about seventy per cent of the population, there are also Russians, Ukrainians, Tajiks, Kazakhs, Tatars, Kara-Kalpaks, Kyrgyz and Koreans. The nation is ninety per cent Muslim, for Islam was brought to Asia in the second half of the seventh century AD, and by the eleventh century had become the dominant religion. Today the country is about ten per cent Christian. While over two million people live in the capital city of Tashkent and some 600,000 in Samarkand, nearly sixty per cent of the population live in the countryside.

This ancient land with its extraordinarily rich culture was relentlessly battered by foreign invasions. For centuries warring conquerors and armies marched through Uzbekistan, building and destroying architectural marvels with equal ease. After Alexander the Great took Samarkand in 329 BC Greek culture flowered in the region, and by the mid-second century BC the Chinese had made the city a center of the Silk Route. With more than a hundred of the Muslim seminaries, *madrassas*, Bukhara was a center of medieval Islamic culture; in the eleventh century the city was home to Avicenna, the famous Arab physician and philosopher. Over the next several hundred years Persian, Hun, Turkish, Chinese and Arab armies swept through the region, and in 1220 in a fierce campaign Genghis Khan sacked Samarkand and Bukhara. More than a hundred years later, in 1370, Tamerlane the Great made Samarkand the capital of his empire. Magnificent gold and blue tiled mosques, and Tamerlane's own mausoleum were built during his reign. In the fifteenth century Tamerlane's grandson, Ulugbek, turned Samarkand into a center for the study of mathematics, the sciences and astronomy, and the Samarkand observatory is world-famous. The name "Uzbek" comes from one of the most outstanding leaders of the Golden Horde, Khan Ozbeg (Uzbek), who reigned in the first half of the fourteenth century. By the eighteenth century Russia had started its advance into Central Asia, and in the nineteenth century the Russian and the British empires were busily engaged in playing what Rudyard Kipling called the "Great Game," seeking adventure, wealth and land. Emirs, khans and princes were simultaneously wooed and warred on, and Uzbekistan became part of the Russian Empire between 1865–1876. It was divided into three states, the Emirate of Bukhara, the Khanates of Kokand, and Khiva. By 1917 two million Russian farmers and tradespeople had moved to Central Asia, and were building their own cities, villages, shops and churches. The year 1921 saw the rise to power of Enver Pasha, an Ottoman Turk who reneged on the initial loyalty he had declared to Lenin and doggedly fought the Bolsheviks with bands of Turk and Tajik guerrilla fighters until his defeat and death in battle in 1922. In the 1920s anti-Soviet guerrilla fighters, the *basmachi*, waged an unsuccessful struggle against Soviet power.

The aftermath of the Red army victory produced the Uzbek Soviet Socialist Republic. While Soviet rule brought progress to the country in the form of a widespread public education system, public health care, and a huge irrigation system, it also subjected Uzbekistan to Russification, an authoritarian system, the rigid grip of farm collectivization, and the appropriation of revenues from the cotton crop, for the country produced seventy per cent of all of the Soviet Union's cotton. Production was so intensive that the rich soil was soon exhausted, and famine spread throughout the country. Thousands of people died resisting collectivization, or perished in the purges of the 1930s.

A huge infrastructure, however, was built during the Soviet era, and the overall standard of living rose considerably. The Arabic script of the Uzbek language, which is related to modern Turkish, was replaced first by a Roman and then by a modified Cyrillic alphabet, and literacy rates rose. The Russian language made great inroads, however, and is still widely spoken today. The Soviet authorities also established a modern, state-run school system. Though in 1966 a huge earthquake badly shattered the capital city of Tashkent, which is today a reconstructed modern urban center, Samarkand and Bukhara continue to preserve the architectural legacy of the past for present and future generations.

With the collapse of the USSR in 1991, Uzbekistan finally became an independent constitutional republic and a full-fledged participant in the international community. Along with the other republics of Central Asia, it became a member state of the United Nations. Nationwide attempts were made to erase the legacy of Soviet rule and to foster the national culture. School programs and textbooks in Uzbek began to replace Russian-language courses and materials, and today the Uzbek language is no longer written in Cyrillic, for it has the same version of the Roman alphabet as that used in Turkey.

The range of nationalities who made up—and continue to make up—the population of the country is vividly reflected in the dazzling and colorful array of powdered spices, dried fruit, fragrant melons and golden breads heaped on the counters of the country's markets. Uzbek food shows the influence of many cultures, for grape leaves from the Middle East, Turkish quinces and lamb dishes, Persian rice pilafs, noodles from China, the flaky pastries of India and composed salads of Russia have all left their mark on Uzbek cuisine. Rice appeared in Central Asia as early as 4,000 BC, and is indispensable for the plovs, stews and soups of Uzbek cooking. The country is studded with colorful stalls and the ubiquitous tea shops (*chaikhana*), the exotic smells and cacaphony of sound of bazaars and cafés, the colorful swirl of brightly colored stripes of the national dress, and the intricate patterns of the embroidered *tubeteika* caps.

While the bazaars and restaurants of Samarkand and Bukhara offer a wealth of tempting delicacies, many of these dishes can be tasted without having to circle the globe, since the preparation of Uzbek specialties does not require rare ingredients, complex utensils, or long hours at the stove. Uzbek hospitality is legendary, and nothing is too good for a guest, be he a close relative or a perfect stranger. Hospitality is sacred and guests, announced or not, are always warmly greeted. *Dastarkhan*, the offering of all kinds of snacks, stuffed pastries, nuts and other treats, is proffered with a smile to every visitor. "God provides for a guest" and "A guest is God's friend" run the Uzbek proverbs. During my first visit to Uzbekistan in 1989, a Bukhara taxi driver who was taking my mother and me back from an ancient mosque to our hotel started up a conversation about the weather which ended with a dinner invitation. Three hours later he returned to the hotel to get us, and by the time we reached his house his wife had managed to prepare a magnificent dinner composed of six salads, a huge lamb *plov*— the national meat and rice based dish, bowls of fruit and sweets, and a platter of freshly baked and gaily decorated *non*, the Uzbek flat bread. Vodka, Uzbek wine, Armenian cognac, fruit syrups diluted with water, and several dozen toasts to international peace and friendship and the health of all present and their absent families and friends accompanied this magnificent and unforgettable dinner.

Food is in evidence everywhere in Uzbekistan, in the hundreds of markets that form commercial and social centers in cities and villages, and in the restaurants and cafes, food stalls and *chaikhana* where men gather for green tea and snacks. Stalls offer stuffed meat and vegetable pies, *plov*, dumplings, and cold drinks, as well as snacks such as salted apricot seeds, roasted chickpeas, puffed wheat and rice, and sugared nuts.

Samarkand and other Uzbek cities pride themselves on a unique institution, the "home restaurant." At midday in certain sections of the old city women descend into the street, smiling at the passersby, and invite them to come up for lunch. They vie with each other in praising their menus of the day and in discussing the price. The visitor who makes an agreement with a hostess is treated as an honored guest in the home, not as a passing client in a restaurant. At a table set with a brightly patterned embroidered tablecloth and the hostess's good crystal and plates, the guest has an extraordinary opportunity to taste home-cooked national dishes, get to know his hosts, or just chat with his friends in a quiet and peaceful atmosphere. The meal we enjoyed in a sun-filled room in Samarkand, with a tender lamb stew, fresh tomato and onion salad, and peaches and grapes of unparalleled sweetness, was far superior to anything the tourist hotels could offer.

Three or four meals a day are customary in Uzbekistan, of which the evening meal, when the heat has subsided, is usually the biggest. For breakfast, tea with milk or cream, rolls and sweets may be served. Lunch is generally a hot meal with salads, soup or a meat dish, and fruit, while an afternoon snack might include a noodle dish, dumplings, tea and sweets. The evening meal features more hot dishes, salads and fruit. Food is ordinarily served on a low table, a *takhta*; a formal meal is served at a higher table. Soup and stews are served from delicate china or ceramic bowls, *kasy*, and tea is served from small china cups, *pialy*, with no handles, which are somewhat similar to Chinese teacups.

Uzbek cooking is primarily based on meat and farinaceous dishes. Lamb is the most widely served meat, the star of many of the several hundred varieties of *plov*. There are also a broad variety of steamed, baked, boiled and fried filled dumplings (*manty*), small stuffed pies (*samsas*), and noodle dishes, accompanied by a wide range of colorful vegetable salads.

Plov (*palov*, in Uzbek, or pilaf, as it is known on the west), is a culinary universal common to most of Asia, Iran,

Azerbaijan and the Middle East, and a close relative of Italian *risottos*. The Greek word *poluv* originally simply meant a varied mixture. Uzbek *plov* allegedly was created when Alexander the Great instructed a soldier to cook a tasty dish from local available ingredients which would be suitable food for warriors, and which the army could easily carry with them. There are *plovs* for any and all occasions, be it a family gathering, a birthday, a wedding, or entertaining guests. Today *plov* is prepared by both men and women, but prior to the Revolution the dish was the domain of male cooks. *Plov*-making is taken very seriously, and boys and girls are taught this art at an early age. Treasured family recipes are handed down from father to son and mother to daughter. Good *plovs* are a source of great local pride, and there are annual *plov*-cooking contests for the best dish.

A *plov* usually consists of meat such as lamb, beef, horse-meat or poultry and a blend of fried carrots and onions (the *zirvak*), rice, and other ingredients that might include mung beans, chickpeas, pumpkin, quince, noodles, nuts, or raisins. The rice for a *plov* is carefully selected from the many varieties available at the market, washed, softened in warm water to plump it, drained and dried. Smoking hot lamb fat is used to sauté the *zirvak* and meat, to which the rice and water are carefully added. The mixture is not stirred, and is cooked slowly until the water has boiled off. After the finished *plov* has been flavored with salt, pepper, cumin and barberries, the rice is piled out onto a large platter and the *zirvak* and other ingredients arranged on top. A variety of side dishes, including tomato, pepper and radish salads, cucumbers and pickles, onion and various greens accompany the *plov*.

Steamed dumplings and buns, fried noodles and mung beans reveal a definite Chinese influence in Uzbek cooking. The impact of Indian cuisine is felt in the use of the Uzbek *tandyr* (Indian *tandoor*) oven, the stuffed pastry *samsas* (Indian samosas), and the *non* flatbreads reminiscent of Indian *nan*. The influence of the Korean population is felt in various types of pickled cabbage (Korean *kim chee*), and other spiced vegetable dishes. Several Korean restaurants in Tashkent offer Korean barbecued meat dishes and a wide variety of other Korean delicacies. As in Azerbaijan, fruit such as apples, quinces, apricots and plums are used in meat dishes and in *plovs*. The heavy use of carrots, however, distinguishes the cooking of Central Asia from that of China or India. Russian soups such as borshch and *shchi* are often found in Uzbek restaurants. The composed salads which are often served as a first course or appetizer are similar to many Russian dishes, and they may be served as side dishes throughout an Uzbek meal as well as for a first course. These consist of cold meat, chicken, or fish, tomatoes, onions, cucumbers, potatoes, carrots or other vegetables, hardboiled eggs, and greens such as parsley, coriander, mint and dill.

Served after the appetizers and before the main course, soups are an important part of an Uzbek meal. These include broths made with noodles, chickpeas (*nut*), mung beans (*mash*), and vegetables. Also popular are milk-based soups laced with herbs, beans and pumpkin.

Pasta is an integral part of Uzbek cuisine, for it was served in Samarkand as early as the thirteenth century. The flavorful national dish, *lagman*, is made from egg noodles, lamb, peppers, and a variety of other ingredients, and depending on its thickness can be served as either a soup or stew. The large steamed or fried *manty* dumplings stuffed with lamb, beef, or vegetables were already being made in the seventeenth century; the smaller boiled *chuchvara* resemble Russian *pelmeni*. Baked or fried round and triangular *samsa* pastries, similar to Russian *pirozhki*, are filled with lamb, lamb fat, onions, chickpeas, potatoes, pumpkin, and various kinds of greens.

Since the country is predominantly Muslim, pork products are not part of the national cuisine. Lamb is the preferred meat, although beef and chicken are also served; fish is less common. Chunks of beef, lamb, liver, chicken and fish are fried, braised in stews, ground, or marinated and grilled in kebab dishes. For *dimlama*, the popular stews consisting of varied combinations of meat, potatoes, onions, vegetables, and fruit, the ingredients are slowly simmered in their own juices.

Though sour milk and cheeses are ingredients in several dishes, Uzbek cooking generally makes less use of dairy products than do the cuisines of some of the other Central Asian countries. *Koumiss* (soured milk), and *ayran*, a salty yogurt and water mixture resembling a thin Russian *kefir*, are popular drinks. *Suzma*, a hard white cheese, is made from yogurt. Balls of dried *suzma*, called *kurtab*, flavored with salt and pepper and left to dry in the sun, are a popular snack sold at many markets. A kind of sweet cream, *qaymak*, is served with honey for breakfast.

Vegetables native to Central Asia commonly found in Uzbek recipes include peppers, pumpkin, carrots, cucumbers, onions, scallions and other greens. Turnips and different kinds of squash are also popular. While relatively new to Uzbek cuisine, tomatoes, potatoes, cabbage, and radishes have become an intrinsic part of the cooking. Though eggplant was cultivated only in the nineteenth century, it is now widely used. Steamed, baked and fried eggplant is an ingredient in various vegetable stews, and is also served as an accompaniment to meat dishes. Mung beans, which are well known to Chinese cuisine, are used in vegetable stews and in gruels with rice, beans, and meat. The tomatoes are fresh and bursting with juice. Since American tomatoes tend to be dry, most of the recipes here suggest the use of canned whole or crushed tomatoes. Should you find vine-ripened juicy ones, however, by all means use them. Uzbek cuisine also includes many ways of preparing stuffed vegetables such as meat and rice-filled cabbage leaves (akin to Russian *golubtsy*), stuffed onions, peppers, tomatoes and quinces, and various kinds of stuffed *dolma* (grape leaves).

The country is rich in fruit, and Uzbekistan's 1,000 varieties of melons are of a sweetness unsurpassed anywhere in the world. Markets overflow with piles of the green and golden globes and watermelons, and with native cherries, pears, plums and apricots. Peaches may have come to Uzbekistan from China, grapes from the Caspian, and figs from the Mediterranean coast or the Arab world. Strawberries, peaches, apples, quinces, persimmons and pomegranates also play an important role in Uzbek cuisine, and numerous varieties of fruit, including melons, and even vegetables such as carrots and tomatoes are made into preserves to accompany tea. For dessert fruit is served fresh and dried, accompanied by an assortment of nuts, or slowly stewed into *kompot*, a dish consisting of the sweetened juice obtained from lengthy simmering of the fruit, served with a few pieces of the cooked fruit.

The flat Uzbek breads, *non*, are an essential part of all meals. Bread is treated with great respect, and crumbs of bread are carefully picked up off the floor. At the start of an Uzbek meal the host takes a flatbread and tears it into pieces, offering a bit to each person present. This ritual of "breaking bread" together serves to unite the people around the table in a bond of fellowship and as a kind of introduction to the meal to come. Baked in a *tandyr* oven, the breads are beautifully decorated with patterns pricked or stamped into the dough. Some are made with lamb fat, onion, sesame seeds, poppy seeds, nigella (a black seed from a flower of the fennel family), or anise. Wheat, corn and chickpea flours are used, and there are plenty of both yeast and unleavened doughs. Breads are mostly baked in a *tandyr* oven, and various kinds of fritters are fried in oil or butter. Water is splashed onto the sides of the oven to create steam, a result which can be replicated by putting a few ice cubes on a heated baking sheet on the bottom of an American oven.

Uzbek desserts include several kinds of halva, dry cookies, sweets made from sugared fruit, baked dry cookies and fried dough pastries. Though some cakes and pastries are borrowed from Russian cooking, this is not a cuisine which has a great many desserts in the western sense of layer cakes, pies, or puddings. Ice cream is frequently served for dessert in restaurants, often on a bed of cracked or dry ice to keep it from melting in the summer heat. Dried fruit, raisins (*kishmish*), and nuts such as walnuts, peanuts, pistachios and almonds are extremely popular, as are dried apricots (*uriuk*). Apricot pits cracked open and cooked in ash until they turn white are a popular snack and are commonly sold at markets and street stands.

Green, and to a lesser extent, black tea are the national drinks. Tea is drunk with meals throughout the day; coffee is not nearly as popular as tea. Traditionally, the *piala* teacup is never filled to the brim. The host refills it as the guest sips, for filling the cup full would be an insult, implying that the guest is to drink up this cup and leave, while pouring out only a little tea signals that more will immediately be offered. Sour milk drinks, fruit juice mixtures and sodas are also widely sold. In Uzbekistan observant Muslims do not drink alcohol, and tea is served throughout the meal; it is a good foil to the fat in meat dishes and in *manty* or *samsa*. Non-observant diners, however, find vodka a good accompaniment to such dishes. Americans, too, may enjoy vodka with the dumplings, but a Cabernet or Chardonnay can also serve as a good accompaniment to many dishes.

A few words should be said about the special cuisine of the Bukhara Jews, Sephardic Jews who have deep roots in Uzbekistan. The twelfth-century Jewish community in Samarkand moved to Bukhara in the sixteenth century following their city's destruction by the Muslims. While many of the foods of the Bukhara Jews are indistinguishable from those of their Muslim neighbors, traditional recipes for chopped liver, fried fish, chicken soup, boiled chicken, nut desserts and Passover recipes using matzo distinguish these dishes from ordinary Uzbek food. Some Ashkenazic Jewish dishes including beef soup and *kholodets*, cold meat in aspic, have also become part of this cuisine.

Though Uzbek cooking makes consistent use of herbs and spices, it does not have the very hot and spicy dishes common to Indian or Thai cuisine. It is no crime to go easy on black or red pepper, and for most of these recipes, except as indicated, the quantities of salt and pepper are a matter of taste. Uzbek cuisine features red and black pepper, cumin seeds, barberries, black and white sesame seeds, nigella, garlic, and herbs such as parsley, coriander, mint, dill, and basil. The cumin seeds which are a part of many fillings for *manty* and *samsas* will release their fragrance when crushed. You can do this by placing the seeds in a small plastic bag and rolling a rolling pin—or even a metal can placed on its side— across them a couple of times. The quantities of herbs such as parsley and coriander used in the recipes can be varied to taste. Vinegar is also used to liven up various dishes, and red wine vinegar or spiced white vinegar is often served on the side along with *samsas* and *manty*. Most of these spices, aside from barberries, are easily available in American stores, and shops specializing in Indian and Pakistani foods carry a wide selection of condiments, and also sell mung beans. The latter can also be found in health food stores. Many recipe ingredients can easily be substituted; you can use lentils instead of mung beans, tart apples instead of quinces, and yogurt instead of sour cream. Canned chickpeas and white beans can be substituted for dried ones.

While most Uzbek dishes do not require unusual or exotic ingredients, a few products are unavailable, while other dishes would not be of interest to most American cooks even if the ingredients could be obtained. Recipes using horsemeat and some subproducts have thus been omitted, as well as dishes based primarily on *kurdiuk*, the lamb fat from the tail of a fat-tailed sheep. *Kurdiuk* is a national delicacy, for when the fat is rendered it forms tiny, crunchy cracklings and sizzling oil which are a part of many dishes, including *plovs*. In solid form it is used for *shashlyks* and as part of the filling for dumplings. In recipes in which *kurdiuk* is used solely for frying or sautéing, it has been replaced by vegetable oil or butter. In Uzbekistan the most popular oils are cottonseed, peanut, and sunflower. You can also use corn oil, but do not use olive oil. This is not used in Uzbek cooking, and will distort the flavors of many dishes. The oil used for sautéing and frying should be very hot, and the onions (plenty of them!) used in many dishes should be sautéed until they are very brown. In recipes with butter, sweet butter should be used unless otherwise indicated.

The procedures for preparing Uzbek dishes do not present any particular difficulties for American cooks. Most foods are steamed, boiled, slowly simmered or braised, grilled or lightly fried; there are not many deep-fried foods. Meat and vegetables should be chopped or sliced as indicated in the recipes. Many soups and stews call for finely sliced or chopped vegetables, and onions are usually cut into semicircular rings. Crushing chopped onions with your hands by pressing them against the bottom of a bowl will make them soften and release their juice, resulting in a more moist *manty* or *samsa* filling. Care should be taken in cutting the meat for Uzbek recipes. For *plovs* meat is usually cut into 1-inch cubes. While Uzbek *samsa* and *manty* recipes often specify "ground" meat, what is actually meant is *very* coarsely ground meat. The meat can be put in the freezer thirty minutes before using, sliced into thin strips and then cut crosswise into ¼-inch cubes. Another way to produce small pieces is to put beef or lamb cut from the shoulder into a food processor and to pulse for a few seconds until the pieces are the size of small peas, but have not formed a mass which sticks together like hamburger meat. For *chuchvara*, the small boiled dumplings, however, the meat should be the consistency of American ground meat. In Uzbekistan the meat used for all of these dishes has a good deal of fat, but lean meat can be used equally well.

The utensils commonly used for Uzbek cooking should not present a problem for the American cook. A metal or a

covered Chinese bamboo steamer, or a double boiler, can substitute for the *mantychnitsa*, the multi-tiered steamer used to prepare *manty*, *chuchvara* and other Uzbek dumplings and steamed buns. The *mantychnitsa* is tightly covered to keep in the steam, which rises to the top through holes in the bottom tier.

A heavy metal pot, Dutch oven or flame-proof casserole can substitute for the heavy *kazan* used to prepare Uzbek *plov*, and a double boiler should be used for preparing steamed stews such as *azhabsanda*. Or a small pot can simply be placed in a large pot filled with a few inches of boiling water. The *parak* or *chekich* used to imprint colorful patterns on the flatbreads can be replaced by a fork. A regular oven will substitute for a *tandyr*, and a charcoal or electrical grill or the oven broiler can replace the Uzbek outdoor grill.

Tandyr ovens in Uzbekistan are both vertical and horizontal. Twigs or stems of the cotton plant are burned to ash, and the walls of the *tandyr* are sprinkled with salt water to prevent the dough from sticking; these heated walls are

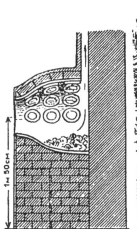

about two centimeters thick. A special mitten, a *panuga*, is worn on the right hand while inserting the dough into the oven, and the bottom of the food is sprayed with water. The cook places the dough pieces on the left wall, working her way to the middle of the ceiling of the *tandyr*. Then using her left hand she covers the walls of the oven from the right wall to the ceiling with the items to be baked.

The Uzbek serving platter, the *lyagan*, is a large plate with raised edges to keep food and sauces from spilling. It also makes for a pretty presentation for *plov* and other meat dishes which have large quantities of sauce. A large shallow bowl or large serving platter makes a good substitute. Deep individual bowls such as those used in Chinese and Japanese restaurants for serving noodle soups can substitute for the Uzbek *kasy* bowls, and small Chinese teacups with no handles can replace the Uzbek *pialy* used for the everpresent black and green tea. Many Chinese stores carry such bowls and cups decorated with blue and white patterns similar to those found on Uzbek chinaware.

Many Uzbek dishes can be successfully prepared and served as part of an American meal. Serving suggestions include American as well as Uzbek dishes which can serve as good accompaniments to many of the recipes, while sample menus suggest choices for an entire Uzbek meal.

While Uzbek food is not well known in the U.S., there are a few places where it can be sampled. The Bukharan Jewish community in the Kew Gardens section of Queens in New York has some ten restaurants packed into an eight-block square area, priding themselves on their *lagman* noodle soup, baked *samsa* meat pies and *manty* dumplings, each convinced that his or hers is better than that served in the neighboring cafe down the block. The owners are well acquainted with many of their guests from the neighborhood, and frequently stop by the tables to chat about families and jobs as well as about the dishes on the menu. The Uzbekistan Tandoori Bread Bakery in Queens, New York, which turns out fluffy *non* breads dotted with black sesame seeds and nigella, and crisp *samsas* under the watchful eye of its owner, Isak Barayev, features a real *tandyr* oven specially brought over from Tashkent. Every day a long line of men (it is they, not the women who are entrusted with the task of buying the freshly baked bread) line up to purchase the fragrant round loaves, exchange news, and sample the salads and tea at the small tables set up in the front of the shop. Shops in the area carry the quinces and eggplants used in many dishes, and Indian and Pakistani shops are filled with the cumin, turmeric, mung beans and rice which are essential for Uzbek cooks. In other parts of Queens, Brooklyn and Manhattan still more Uzbek restaurants provide emigres with a taste of home and New Yorkers with an introduction to an exotic cuisine.

Another source for Uzbek cuisine is Seattle, Washington, since 1973 the sister city of the Uzbek capital, Tashkent. Seattle, in fact, was the first U.S. city to acquire a Soviet sister city affiliation. Many of the local citizens have hosted visitors from Uzbekistan or visited the capital, and have actively helped to build parks in Tashkent and provide medical assistance. The two cities have established programs for school, physician, and graphic arts exchanges, as well as exchanges between the Jewish communities. The Seattle Sister Cities cookbook includes Uzbek recipes, and I am most grateful to Joyce Doan, Lydia Barrett and Anne Stadler for their advice, recollections of food in Uzbekistan, and for permission to adapt some of the sister city recipes. Isak Barayev of the Uzbekistan Tandoori Bread Bakery in New York graciously provided some of his recipes. Boris Elyukin, his wife Elena Granovskiy, Valeriy Granovskiy and other family members were generous with their family recipes, time, and culinary advice. I am also deeply grateful to Anya von Bremzen and Darra Goldstein, two specialists on the cooking of Russia and the countries of the former Soviet Union, for permission to adapt recipes from their cookbooks, and to Dalia Carmel for her most valuable assistance. And special thanks go to George Blagowidow at Hippocrene Publishers for his enthusiasm for this project, and to Carol Chitnis for her unfailingly patient and cheerful editorial assistance. Translation systems for rendering Uzbek names into English vary, and there may be inconsistencies in rendering some of the names.

May these recipes whet your appetite to see for yourself the ancient marvels of Uzbekistan, the gorgeous mosques and minarets of Bukhara and Samarkand, the colorful markets of Tashkent, and the modern development and progress of a vibrant society with ancient roots and customs.

APPETIZERS
AND
SALADS

The salads which cover the table at the beginning of an Uzbek meal include colorful mixtures of raw, boiled, marinated and pickled vegetables such as cucumbers, red and white radishes, tomatoes, scallions, mushrooms and turnips, and dishes made with eggs, cold meat, chicken, and fish. These composed salads are sprinkled with parsley, dill or coriander, and are lightly bound with mayonnaise, sour cream, or vinegar and oil. The quantity of dressing should be just enough to bind the salad, but not to drown the ingredients. In Uzbekistan some salads are served highly seasoned, but you can adjust the salt and pepper to taste.

Most of the ingredients used in these salads are readily available. Pomegranate seeds and white radish (daikon) can be found in many oriental vegetable markets or stores. If you cannot find something, don't hesitate to substitute ingredients by replacing white radishes with red ones or by using a hard goat cheese instead of Feta cheese. While many dishes use the fresh vegetables and fruit which are indigenous to Uzbekistan such as red and white radishes, onions, carrots, cucumbers and scallions, the influence of Russian cuisine is felt in the use of mayonnaise and in some of the composed meat and vegetable salads. The Korean population in Uzbekistan has contributed the *Shim sha* (Korean *kim chee*) spicy cabbage salad sold at Uzbek markets, and spiced carrots are served both as an appetizer and as an accompaniment to main dishes.

An unwary guest may well mistake a table covered with colorful salads for the entire meal, and have no room for the soup and meat dishes which follow. There is no need to rush to try all the salads right away, since many of the dishes remain on the table to accompany a *plov*, dumplings or other main dish. It is almost always possible to catch up with a dish you missed or to have a second helping!

Flatbread is served along with the salads, and remains on the table for the rest of the meal. Shots of vodka or a light, dry white wine go well with these dishes. While most of the salads should be served at room temperature, as excessive cold will dull the flavors, be sure to keep salads made with mayonnaise or sour cream dressings refrigerated until 30 minutes before serving time, especially in summer.

For American dinners, a combination of small portions of these appetizers and salads can make for an interesting first course. Cucumber and radish salad contrasts nicely with cheese-stuffed peppers, and white radish and pomegranate salad goes well with a fish or chicken-based salad. Some of the dishes, such as the *lovia* bean salad or the potato salad could also be served with a main course such as *shashlyk* or grilled chicken, or with American cold meat or fish main courses.

The servings given for the recipes are for appetizer-size portions, but many of the meat and chicken-based salad recipes when doubled can serve as luncheon main courses. Suggestions for accompaniments to the salads include both Western and Uzbek dishes.

You can use the chopping blade of a food processor to cut most of the ingredients into the very small pieces required by many recipes, but be careful not to reduce the pieces to crumb size or to purée them. Do not add the dressing too far in advance of serving a salad containing radishes, as they will give off water and make the salad soggy. Fresh herbs are always preferable to dried ones, but if no fresh ones are available and you are using dried herbs reduce the quantity appropriately.

❦ BUKHARAN CHOPPED LIVER PÂTÉ
(Kima az chigari)

¾ pound beef or calf liver
½ cup vegetable oil
1 medium onion, peeled and coarsely chopped
1 medium potato, peeled and diced into ½-inch cubes
Salt to taste
Freshly ground black pepper
2 hard-boiled eggs, peeled and chopped
1 tablespoon minced dill

Clean the liver by removing the membrane and cut it into 1-inch cubes.

Place the cubes in an oven-proof casserole, salt them, and broil for two to three minutes. Remove from the oven.

In a heavy frying pan heat the oil, add the onions, and brown till onions start turning golden.

Add the potato, and continue frying for 5 minutes over low to medium heat.

Add the liver, stirring constantly, and when it starts to brown reduce the heat.

Sprinkle the mixture with salt and pepper, and cook on low heat for 15 minutes. If mixture starts to burn add a little more oil.

Add the eggs and stir well for 2–3 minutes. Remove from heat and pour off any excess oil.

Cool slightly and process until blended, taking care that the mixture does not become too liquid or too smooth; it should retain a slightly rough texture.

Taste for seasoning and add salt and pepper as needed.

Chill and sprinkle with dill before serving. The dish should be served at room temperature.

Makes approximately 2–2½ cups.
Serves 4–6 as a first course.

The pâté can be served with crackers as a cocktail snack or over lettuce leaves, garnished with a combination of sliced hardboiled eggs, chopped parsley, and tomato wedges.

CHEESE-STUFFED PEPPERS
(Lazzat appetizer)

4 large Italian sweet peppers
1 pound Feta cheese
3 tablespoons sour cream
1 tablespoon softened butter or margarine
1 clove garlic, crushed
2 tablespoons finely chopped dill

Carefully remove the seeds from the peppers, and cut them in half crosswise.

Place the peppers in a sieve and sprinkle them with boiling water, or parboil for 30 seconds in boiling water.

Mash the Feta cheese well and blend in the sour cream, butter or margarine, garlic and dill. Do not use a food processor or blend to a purée; the mixture should be well blended but uneven in texture.

Stuff the pepper halves with the cheese and arrange on a plate. To serve, cut the peppers crosswise to form thin slices.

Makes 8 pepper halves, approximately 32 slices.

The pepper slices can be served on crackers or thin slices of pumpernickel with drinks, or with a few other salads as appetizers. They are also a good accompaniment to cold meat and fish dishes.

❧ TOMATO AND CUCUMBER SALAD
(Achchik-chuchuk)

4 large ripe tomatoes, sliced
2 medium onions, peeled and thinly sliced
4 Kirby cucumbers, peeled and thinly sliced
Salt to taste
Freshly ground black pepper
Pinch cayenne pepper (optional)
3 tablespoons red wine vinegar
4 teaspoons vegetable oil

Combine all the vegetables and sprinkle with salt, black pepper and the cayenne, if you are using it.

Add the vinegar and oil and toss gently.

Refrigerate for an hour before serving, and serve at room temperature.

Serves 6.

This is a very popular dish in Uzbekistan and is served as part of a series of appetizer salads, with *plovs*, and with *shashlyks*.

❦ SPRING SALAD
(Salat vesennii)

(Courtesy of Boris Elyukin)

1 bunch red radishes (about 10 large radishes), thinly sliced
7 scallions, diced (green parts only)
1 Kirby cucumber, peeled and diced
5 large lettuce leaves (such as Boston lettuce), shredded
1 teaspoon salt
1 tablespoon mayonnaise
2 tablespoons sour cream

Combine the radishes, scallions, cucumber and lettuce.

Sprinkle in the salt.

Combine the mayonnaise and sour cream, and stir into the vegetables.

Serves 4–5.

Do not dress the salad more than 30 minutes in advance of serving, as the radishes will give off water and make the other vegetables soggy.

🌿 CUCUMBER AND RADISH SALAD
(Navruz salat)

1 small head of lettuce, such as Boston lettuce
2 Kirby cucumbers, peeled, seeded and finely chopped
8 radishes, cleaned and diced
3 scallions (white and green parts), diced
2 hard-boiled eggs, peeled and coarsely chopped
⅓ cup sour cream
2 tablespoons chopped fresh dill
2 tablespoons chopped fresh parsley
2 tablespoons chopped fresh coriander
Salt and pepper
3 tablespoons coarsely grated Muenster cheese

Wash lettuce and tear it into small pieces.

Add the cucumbers, radishes, scallions and eggs, and stir in the sour cream, blending until mixture is smooth.

Stir in dill, parsley and coriander, and add salt and pepper to taste.

Place salad in a bowl and sprinkle with the cheese.

Serves 4–6.

Note: If you are not going to serve the salad immediately, mix together all the ingredients except for the cheese and sour cream. If the sour cream is added too long before serving time the radishes and cucumbers will start giving off water, and the salad will be soggy. If you are preparing the dish in advance, add the sour cream at the last minute and then sprinkle with the cheese.

🦫 RADISH AND EGG SALAD
(Rediska salati)

8 large red radishes, cleaned and chopped
½ white radish (daikon), peeled and grated
3 scallions (green and white parts), chopped
3 hard-boiled eggs, peeled, cooled and coarsely chopped
2 tablespoons chopped fresh parsley
2 tablespoons chopped fresh coriander
Salt and freshly ground black pepper
⅓ cup yogurt (approximately)

Combine the red and white radishes, scallions and eggs; stir in the parsley and coriander.

Sprinkle with salt and pepper to taste.

About 20 minutes before serving stir in the yogurt. (If you do this earlier the radishes will start giving off liquid and the salad will be watery). Add the yogurt, using just enough to bind the mixture; it should not become soupy.

Serves 4.

This salad makes a nice lunch dish when served with sliced cold meats and cheeses, and fresh fruit for dessert.

❧ WHITE RADISH AND CARROT SALAD
(Rediska va sabzi salati)

(Courtesy of Boris Elyukin)

2 cups coarsely grated white radish (daikon) (use the
    largest holes on the grater)
2 cups coarsely grated carrots (use the largest holes on
    the grater)
1 medium potato, peeled, boiled, and coarsely diced
1 teaspoon salt
1 tablespoon mayonnaise
2 tablespoons sour cream

Combine the radish, carrots, potato, and salt, taking care
not to mash the potato.

Blend the mayonnaise and sour cream. Stir into the vegetables, blending well.

Serves 4–5

❧ WHITE RADISH AND POMEGRANATE SALAD
(Anor donasi bilan turpli salat)

1 large white radish (daikon), peeled
1 large pomegranate
1 large carrot
1 teaspoon red wine vinegar
½–1 teaspoon sugar
Salt
1 tablespoon chopped fresh parsley

Grate the white radish, using the large holes of a grater. Allow the grated radish to sit for 10 minutes, and pour off about half of the accumulated liquid.

Cut the pomegranate in half and gently squeeze the seeds from the two halves into the radish. (Note: Be very careful in handling the pomegranate, as stains from this fruit are nearly impossible to remove from clothing! Be sure to wear an apron.)

Peel the carrot and grate it into the radish mixture.

Add the vinegar and sugar. How much sugar you put in will depend on how sweet you like the salad, though the final product should be tart.

Season with salt to taste.

Refrigerate for 30 minutes. Just before serving sprinkle with the fresh parsley.

Serves 4.

This is an excellent accompaniment to *shashlyk* or *plov* dishes. It also goes nicely with omelets and other egg dishes.

🌸 WHITE RADISH AND ALMOND SALAD
(Turp va enfokli salat)

1 cup grated white radish (daikon)
¾ cup slivered blanched almonds
1 medium pomegranate
1 teaspoon red wine vinegar
1 teaspoon sugar

Pat the grated radish dry with a paper towel to remove excess moisture. Stir in the almonds, and mix well.

Cut the pomegranate in half (be careful not to stain your clothes!) and gently squeeze the seeds from the halves into the radish mixture.

Squeeze in the pomegranate juice, and add the vinegar and sugar. Chill for at least 1 hour.

Serves 4.

This goes well with meat and chicken salads, or as an accompaniment to grilled meat.

🌸 WHITE RADISH AND CHEESE SALAD
(Turp va sir salati)

2 cups white radish (daikon), peeled and cut into 1-inch
    strips (about ½ of 1 large radish)
¾ pound Muenster cheese, cut into 1-inch long thin strips
Salt and freshly ground black pepper

Combine the radish and the cheese strips in a bowl, taking care not to mash the cheese. Sprinkle with salt and pepper to taste, and refrigerate for 40 minutes. Serve at room temperature.

This is a good side dish for a *plov* or other lamb dishes, or for stews.

Serves 4–5.

🌿 RED ONION SALAD WITH POMEGRANATE SEEDS
(*Anor va pioz salati*)

4 large red onions
Salt
1¼ cups pomegranate seeds
⅓ cup red wine vinegar
1½ teaspoons sugar
4 plum tomatoes (optional), coarsely chopped
¾ cup minced fresh coriander

Peel the onions, slice them into thin rings and cut the rings in half.

Place them in a colander and sprinkle with 2 teaspoons salt.

Toss well, place a plate under the colander to hold the liquid that will drain off, and allow to stand for 30 minutes.

Drain off any remaining liquid from the onions in the colander, and then pat them dry with a paper towel.

Stir in the pomegranate seeds, the vinegar, sugar, and, if you are using them, the tomatoes. (Some recipes for this salad do not include tomatoes, but they provide a nice taste and color contrast).

Taste for seasoning and add salt or sugar if you wish. The salad should have a sweetish-tart flavor.

Refrigerate the salad for two hours, and serve at room temperature.

Just before serving sprinkle with coriander and toss well.

Serves 8.

This dish is an excellent accompaniment to *plovs* and *shashlyks*.

🌿 TURNIP AND CHICKPEA SALAD
(Sholgom va nuikhat salati)

3 medium turnips, peeled
2 carrots, peeled
1 medium onion, peeled
1½ cups cooked chickpeas, drained
Salt and freshly ground pepper
½ cup sour cream

Cut the turnips into quarters and the carrots into 2-inch long pieces, and cook both vegetables in boiling salted water for 10 minutes.

Cool, and cut into ½-inch cubes.

Parboil the onion by immersing it in boiling water for 1 minute, and then cut it into thin rings.

Combine the turnips, carrots, onion and chickpeas, and add salt and pepper to taste.

Blend in the sour cream and chill the salad for 20 minutes in the refrigerator.

Serves 6.

This is good with cold fish or chicken, or with grilled meats.

❦ TURNIP AND MUSHROOM SALAD
(Sholgom va kuizkorin salati)

2 medium turnips, peeled and quartered
1 carrot, peeled and cut into 2-inch strips
2 tablespoons butter
8 ounces mushrooms, washed and coarsely chopped
2 small dill pickles, chopped
Salt and freshly ground black pepper
½ teaspoon dried mint or 1 teaspoon chopped fresh mint
2 tablespoons chopped fresh coriander
3 tablespoons sour cream

Put turnips and carrots into a pot with just enough water to cover, and bring to a boil.

Reduce the heat and cook until tender but not mushy, about 10 minutes.

In a separate pan melt the butter and sauté the mushrooms until soft and slightly browned, about 5–7 minutes.

Drain the mushrooms, preserving their liquid.

Drain the turnips and carrots, and cut them into ½-inch cubes.

Place them in a bowl and add the mushrooms, pickles, salt and pepper to taste, mint and coriander.

Add 2 tablespoons of the liquid from the mushrooms; if there is more, discard it. Stir in the sour cream and blend well.

Chill for an hour, and serve at room temperature.

Serves 4.

The salad can be served on lettuce leaves, garnished with wedges of hard-boiled eggs. Black bread and a shot of vodka make nice accompaniments.

🦎 KOREAN CARROT SALAD
(Uzbek style)

4 large carrots, peeled and cut into very thin 2-inch long
    julienne strips
2 scallions, trimmed and finely chopped (green and
    white parts)
1 clove garlic, peeled and minced
2½ tablespoons soy sauce
1 tablespoon white vinegar
1½ tablespoons white sesame seeds
1½ tablespoons sesame oil
1 teaspoon sugar
Pinch chili powder
Pinch cayenne pepper

Boil 4 cups water and drop in the carrots. Cook for 4 minutes and remove from heat.

Drain and cool the carrots.

Combine all remaining ingredients and stir until the sugar has dissolved and the dressing is well blended.

Pour over the carrots, and serve at room temperature.

Makes about 3 cups.

Serve as a side dish to *shashlyk* and grilled chicken, or as part of a group of appetizers. This salad can also be served on lettuce leaves, garnished with with fresh tomatoes and cucumbers.

🦁 CABBAGE AND APPLE SALAD
(Oltin kuz salat)

5–6 cups shredded cabbage
1½ tablespoons sugar
1 teaspoon lemon juice
2 apples, peeled, cored and chopped
3–4 tablespoons mayonnaise
Salt
¼ cup coarsely chopped walnuts
3 tablespoons coarsely grated Swiss cheese

In a large bowl sprinkle the cabbage with the sugar and lemon juice, and mix well.

Add apples and mayonnaise, and sprinkle with salt to taste.

Form the salad into a mound and refrigerate until time to serve.

Just before serving sprinkle with the walnuts and cheese.

Serves 6.

This salad is good with *shashlyks* or grilled fish. It can be garnished with wedges of tomato and hard-boiled egg.

❧ CABBAGE AND VEGETABLE SALAD
(Karam salati)

(Adapted from Darra Goldstein, *The Vegetarian Hearth:* Harper Collins Publishers, New York, 1996)

2½ tablespoons vegetable oil
1 small onion, peeled and minced
1 garlic clove, peeled and crushed
1 cup shredded cabbage
5 large radishes, diced
Salt and pepper to taste
2½ tablespoons tomato paste
2 tablespoons chopped fresh parsley
2 tablespoons chopped fresh dill

In a small frying pan heat 1½ tablespoons of the oil, and fry the onion and garlic until the vegetables are soft.

Drain off any excess oil and allow to cool.

Blend the cabbage, radishes, garlic and onion mixture, and season with salt and pepper to taste.

In a small bowl beat the remaining tablespoon of oil with the tomato paste. Stir into the vegetables and blend well.

Sprinkle with the parsley and dill just before serving.

Serves 4.

This goes well with egg dishes or with meat *samsas*; it can also stand alone as a salad course, served on lettuce leaves.

🌿 KOREAN CABBAGE
(Shim sha/Kim chee)

Though this dish is originally Korean, it is sold at Uzbek markets and is often found on restaurant menus in Uzbekistan and in Uzbek restaurants in the U.S. The salad is slightly less spicy and oily than in Korean recipes.

1 head Chinese bok choy or white cabbage, cut into strips 2-inches and about ½-inch wide
¾ pound white radish, peeled and cut into very thin, 1½-inch long strips
8 scallions, finely diced
4 tablespoons salt
2 cloves garlic, peeled and minced
1 stalk celery, shredded
Piece of 1-inch long fresh ginger, peeled and diced
1 pear (not too ripe), peeled, cored, and cut into 1-inch long thin strips
2 teaspoons chili powder
1 tablespoon sugar
¾ teaspoon cayenne pepper

Combine the cabbage, white radish, scallions and salt, and allow to rest for 5–6 hours or overnight.

Place in a colander or large strainer, and rinse well with cold water. Add all the other ingredients, and mix well.

Put the salad in a bowl, place a plate on top of it and put a weight on the plate. Allow the cabbage to chill for at least 2 days in the refrigerator.

Makes about 5 cups.

This is a good contrast to blander salads in an array of appetizers, or as a complement to *shashlyk* or steaks.

🌱 BEAN SALAD
(Lovia salati)

1½ cups cooked white beans (if using canned beans, drain
    and rinse well)
1 large onion, peeled and diced
1 large carrot, peeled and diced
1 clove garlic, peeled and diced
Salt and pepper to taste
¼ cup chopped fresh coriander
¼ cup chopped fresh parsley
1½ tablespoons red wine vinegar
2½ tablespoons vegetable oil
Lettuce leaves

In a bowl combine the beans, onion, carrot, garlic, and sprinkle with salt and pepper to taste.

Add the coriander and parsley, and blend in the vinegar and oil.

Allow the mixture to rest at room temperature for 30 minutes.

Serve on lettuce leaves.

Serves 6.

This salad can accompany a wide variety of meat dishes, *shashlyks*, or broiled or grilled chicken. It contrasts well with chicken or radish salads.

🦁 BEAN AND VEGETABLE SALAD
(Sabzavot va dukkak makhsulotli salat)

3 turnips, peeled and quartered
2 carrots, peeled and quartered
1 medium onion, peeled and finely chopped
1½ cups cooked white beans, drained
Salt and pepper
½ cup sour cream
2 tablespoons chopped fresh dill

Boil the turnips and carrots for 10–12 minutes, drain, cool, and cut into ½-inch cubes.

Add the onion and beans, and sprinkle with salt and pepper to taste.

Blend the sour cream with the dill and combine with the vegetables.

Chill for 30 minutes.

Serves 6.

This salad goes well with egg dishes or with meat and chicken salads.

POTATO SALAD
(Salat yangalik)

4 large potatoes, peeled, boiled and diced
½ cup cooked peas
2 carrots, peeled, boiled and diced
1 small onion, peeled and finely chopped
4 small dill pickles (gherkins), diced (about ¾ cup)
2 tablespoons chopped fresh parsley
2 tablespoons chopped fresh dill
2 tablespoons chopped fresh coriander
Salt and pepper
¼ cup (approximately) vegetable oil

Blend the potatoes, peas, carrots, onion and pickles together gently, taking care not to mash the potatoes.

Add the parsley, dill and coriander, and sprinkle with salt and pepper to taste.

Slowly stir in the oil; you should use just enough to bind the ingredients together.

Allow the salad to sit for 30 minutes at room temperature before serving.

Serves 6.

This salad can be served on lettuce leaves, garnished with wedges of hard-boiled eggs, cucumber slices, or sliced scallions, as a first course, a lunch main course, with flatbread or a loaf of garlic bread on the side.

❧ WHITE CHEESE SALAD
(Suzmali kujk salat)

¾ pound Feta cheese
½ cup sour cream
2 Kirby cucumbers, peeled and chopped
⅔ cup white radish (daikon), peeled and grated, or
    8 red radishes, chopped
3 scallions, white and green part, chopped
¼ cup chopped fresh parsley
¼ cup chopped fresh coriander
1 tablespoon minced dill
1 teaspoon cumin seeds
Salt
Pinch cayenne pepper

Crumble the Feta cheese into pieces the size of small peas, and stir in the sour cream, mixing with a wooden spoon until smooth. Be careful not to mash the cheese.

Stir in the cucumbers, radishes, and scallions, and then blend in the parsley, coriander, dill and cumin.

Sprinkle in salt sparingly; the amount you need will depend on the saltiness of the Feta cheese. Add cayenne to taste, stir well, and chill.

Serves 6–8.

This salad can be served on romaine or iceberg lettuce leaves, garnished with fresh tomato wedges, as a first course, or as part of a set of appetizers.

🌿 TASHKENT MEAT SALAD
(Tashkent salati)

1 tablespoon butter
1 small onion, peeled and cut into 1-inch long julienne
½ cup white radish (daikon), peeled and cut into
    1-inch long julienne
¼ pound beef or lamb, boiled and cut into1-inch
    long julienne
3 large red radishes, trimmed and thinly sliced
Salt and freshly ground black pepper
2 tablespoons chopped fresh dill
2 tablespoons chopped fresh Italian flat-leaf parsley
2 tablespoons chopped fresh coriander
3–4 tablespoons mayonnaise
1 hard-boiled egg, peeled and thinly sliced
2 tablespoons scallions, minced

In a small frying pan heat the butter until it is very hot, and add the onion.

Cook, stirring over medium high heat for 4–5 minutes until the onion is well browned.

Pour off any remaining butter and drain the onion on paper towels.

Cool it to room temperature.

Place the white radish strips in a bowl of cold water and let them sit for 10–15 minutes.

Drain well.

Combine the meat, onion, white and red radishes, and sprinkle with salt and pepper to taste.

Add the dill, parsley and coriander and mix well.

Blend in enough mayonnaise to bind the salad (about 3–4 tablespoons), mound in a bowl and refrigerate.

Serve garnished with the sliced egg and scallions.

Serves 3 as an appetizer or side dish.

The fried onion gives this salad a unique flavor. The recipe can be doubled or tripled to serve as a lunch dish, accompanied by a tomato and cucumber salad.

🌿 MEAT AND CABBAGE SALAD
(Salat andizhan)

¼ pound boiled beef or lamb, cut into thin 1-inch strips
⅓ cup white radish, cut into 1-inch julienne
1 carrot, peeled, parboiled and cut into 1-inch julienne
⅔ cup cabbage, shredded
1 Kirby cucumber, peeled and cut into 1-inch julienne
1 hard-boiled egg, peeled and chopped
2 tablespoons chopped fresh Italian flat-leaf parsley
Salt
3–4 tablespoons mayonnaise

In a bowl combine the meat, radish, carrots, cabbage, cucumber, egg and parsley.

Sprinkle with salt to taste.

Blend in enough mayonnaise to hold the mixture together, taking care not to crush the vegetables.

Refrigerate for 30 minutes.

Serves 4.

The salad can be garnished with additional chopped parsley, sliced carrots, and sliced hard-boiled egg. The recipe can be doubled and served as a lunch main dish.

🌿 MEAT AND VEGETABLE SALAD
(Salat bakhor)

½ pound boiled lamb or beef, sliced into 1-inch long
    thin strips
3 Kirby cucumbers, peeled and sliced into 1-inch long
    thin strips
2 tomatoes, thinly sliced
2 scallions, white and green parts, minced
Salt and freshly ground black pepper
1 small clove garlic, peeled and finely minced
1 tablespoon chopped fresh dill
1 tablespoon chopped fresh coriander
2 tablespoons red wine vinegar
1 tablespoon vegetable oil
3 tablespoons mayonnaise
1 hard-boiled egg, peeled and sliced

In a bowl combine the lamb, cucumbers, tomatoes, and scallions, and sprinkle lightly with salt and pepper.

In a separate small bowl combine the garlic, dill, coriander, vinegar and oil.

Combine the vinegar and oil mixture with the meat and vegetables. Taste for salt and pepper, and adjust seasoning as needed.

Blend in the mayonnaise, taking care not to crush the vegetables.

Mound the mixture in a bowl. If the salad is not to be served immediately, chill and remove from refrigerator 20 minutes before serving.

Decorate with slices of the hard-boiled egg.

Serves 4.

This salad is good as a main dish; it can also be served with a pasta salad or warm flatbread or garlic bread.

🦁 GULISTON CHICKEN SALAD
(Salat Guliston)

1 cup cold chicken, skinned, boned, and cut into thin strips
1 cup grated white radish (daikon) or 8 red radishes, diced
1 cup cooked peas
1 quince (or tart apple, if quince is not available)
2 hard-boiled eggs, peeled
1 small onion, peeled and finely chopped
¼ cup chopped fresh parsley
¼ cup chopped fresh coriander
1 tablespoon chopped fresh basil
Salt and freshly ground black pepper
¼ cup mayonnaise (approximately)

Blend the chicken with the radishes and peas.

Peel, core and cut the quince or apple into large dice and bring it to a boil in water to cover; if using the apple cook for 4–5 minutes over medium low heat, and if using the quince, for 20–25 minutes, until soft.

Drain the pieces, cool them briefly, and add to the mixture.

Chop 1 hard-boiled egg coarsely and blend into the salad.

Stir in the onion, parsley, coriander, basil and salt and pepper to taste.

Fold in the mayonnaise, adding more if needed to bind the mixture, and taste again for seasoning.

Chill for at least 1 hour before serving. Quarter the remaining hard-boiled egg and use it to garnish the salad.

Serves 4–6.

This salad can be served as a main dish with a tomato-cucumber salad on the side. It is also good with omelets.

❧ CHICKEN AND VEGETABLE SALAD
(Zarafshan salat)

¾ pound chicken breast, cooked and diced
2 large potatoes, peeled and diced
2 hard-boiled eggs, peeled
2 tablespoons mayonnaise
Salt and freshly ground black pepper
1 Kirby cucumber, peeled and sliced
2 plum tomatoes, sliced
2 tablespoons minced coriander
2 scallions (green part), minced

Carefully blend chicken with potatoes, taking care not to mash the potatoes.

Coarsely chop one of the hard-boiled eggs and add to the mixture.

Fold in mayonnaise and sprinkle with salt and pepper to taste.

Mound salad on a plate.

Slice the second hard-boiled egg.

Cover the salad with a decorative pattern of tomato, cucumber and egg slices.

Sprinkle with minced coriander and scallions.

Serve at room temperature.

Serves 4.

This salad can also be served as a main dish, or as an accompaniment to an omelet or soufflé.

FISH SALAD
(Balikli salat)

¾ pound cooked fish fillets (hake, cod, scrod or other fish), boned and flaked
4 large boiled potatoes, peeled and diced
2 large carrots, peeled, boiled and diced
½ clove garlic, peeled and crushed (optional)
2 hard-boiled eggs, peeled and coarsely chopped
1 small onion, peeled and chopped
1 small dill pickle, diced
2 Kirby cucumbers, peeled, seeded and diced
1 teaspoon minced dill
1 teaspoon minced parsley
Salt and freshly ground black pepper
4–5 tablespoon mayonnaise

Combine the fish with the potatoes, carrots, garlic, eggs, onion, pickle, and cucumbers, blending carefully so as not to mash the fish and potatoes.

Sprinkle with half of the dill and parsley, and with salt and pepper to taste. Be careful with the salt, as the salt content will vary depending on the kind of fish you are using, and the pickle is also salty.

Carefully fold in mayonnaise, and shape into a mound.

Sprinkle with remaining dill and parsley, and chill.

Serves 6–8.

This salad can be served as a main dish, accompanied by warm flatbread or garlic bread, and a fresh tomato or string bean salad. It also goes well with a quiche or omelet.

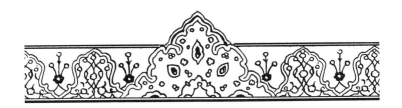

SOUPS

Uzbek cooking features a wide variety of soups. One of the most famous national dishes, the *lagman* lamb and noodle soup, has so many ingredients and is so thick that it closely resembles a stew. Do not make a heavy main course when you are serving this dish! Few people today have time to make the traditional noodles which go into the soup, but store-bought egg noodles or spaghetti will do fine.

Beef and lamb soups with pasta are also common winter fare. In almost all of the soup recipes, beef and lamb can be used interchangeably. Do not hesitate to use beef or chicken cubes dissolved in water if you have no broth, but add seasoning carefully, since the cubes may be quite salty. The meat for *lagman* and most other soups should be cut into very small cubes (½-inch at most). Carrots are usually cut in coarse julienne rather than into rounds. Uzbek soups are generally nicely spiced but not searingly hot, so feel free to adjust the salt and pepper to taste.

Rice soup, *mastava*, is a national favorite, as are soups made with *mash* (mung beans), which are simmered with rice and meat into thick purées. Though the mung beans in most Uzbek recipes do not have to be presoaked, it will take about 35–40 minutes of simmering in the soup for them to open and pop. If you do soak them overnight they will soften after about 15 minutes of cooking. If there are no mung beans, lentils can be substituted, but reduce the quantity by about one-third.

A *shurpa* is a nourishing hot soup combining meat and vegetables cut into fairly large pieces, while a dairy-based cold soup, *chalop*, made of sour milk and a variety of finely chopped green vegetables, provides refreshing relief from the broiling summer sun.

It is always advisable to skim the fat from the soup, particularly when you are dealing with larger quantities of meat. The best way to do this is to chill the soup in the refrigerator for a couple of hours or overnight until the fat congeals on the top, but if you don't have time you can skim it from the surface. Soups are usually served sprinkled with finely minced parsley, dill or coriander or with a dollop of yogurt or sour cream. Even if herbs such as chopped parsley or coriander have already been added during cooking, you can always sprinkle the tureen or each bowl with a bit more just before serving.

When accompanied by Uzbek flatbread or a crusty French bread, salad and fruit, many of the thick meat soups can make a filling one-dish meal.

🦎 MEAT AND VEGETABLE SOUP
(Mastava)

3 tablespoons vegetable oil
1 pound beef or lamb for stew, cut into ¼-inch cubes
    (these should be very small!)
1 small onion, peeled and cut into semicircular rings
1 large carrot, peeled and diced
1 large turnip, peeled and diced
3 tablespoons tomato paste
6 cups water
Salt and freshly ground black pepper to taste
1 large potato, peeled and diced
¾ cup rice
¼ cup chopped fresh coriander + 2 tablespoons
    for garnish
Sour cream

Heat the oil until it is very hot and add the meat, stirring over medium high heat until it is browned on all sides.

Add the onion, carrot, and turnip, reduce the heat to medium, and cook for 5–7 minutes, stirring constantly, until the vegetables are soft but not brown.

Stir in the tomato paste and mix well. Slowly pour in the water, cup by cup, stirring to produce a smooth mixture.

Raise the heat and bring the soup to a boil.

Add salt and pepper to taste (the soup will need a good dose of both), stir in the potato and sprinkle in the rice.

Lower the heat, partially cover, and simmer for 20 minutes. Taste for seasoning, and add salt and pepper as needed. Add the ¼ cup coriander.

Ladle the soup into bowls, sprinkle each with some of the remaining coriander, and serve with sour cream on the side.

Serves 6–8.

With a green salad and flatbread on the side, this soup makes a good one-dish meal.

❦ MEAT, MUNG BEAN AND RICE SOUP
(Mashkhurda)

2 tablespoons vegetable oil
½ pound lamb or beef, cut into ½-inch cubes
½ medium onion, peeled and cut in semicircular rings
1 carrot, peeled and diced
6 cups water
½ cup mung beans, washed and picked over
3 tablespoons tomato paste (optional)
⅓ cup rice
1 medium potato, peeled and diced
Salt and freshly ground black pepper
1 scallion (green part), diced
Yogurt

Heat the oil in a skillet until it is very hot, and add the meat. Fry the meat quickly over high heat, turning all the pieces to be sure they are well browned.

Put in the onion and carrot and continue to fry on medium high heat for about 5 minutes, stirring constantly to keep the mixture from burning.

Remove the mixture to a pot and pour in the water. Bring to a boil and add the beans.

Partially cover the pot and simmer on low heat for about 40 minutes, until the beans open.

Blend in the tomato paste (if you are using it), the rice, and potato, and cook, covered, on medium heat for 15 minutes.

Add salt and pepper to taste and cook for another 5 minutes. Skim off any fat on the surface.

Ladle the soup into bowls and sprinkle each portion with a few pieces of scallion, and place a dollop of yogurt in the center of each serving.

Serves 6–8.

With a green salad and/or omelet, flatbread or garlic bread, this soup can serve as a one-dish meal.

🌿 MEAT, MUNG BEAN AND NOODLE SOUP
(Mash ugra)

2 tablespoons vegetable oil
½ pound lamb or beef, cut into ½-inch cubes
1 small onion, peeled and cut in semicircular rings
1 carrot, peeled and diced
7 cups water
½ cup mung beans, washed and picked over
1 medium potato, peeled and diced
⅔ cup cooked thin egg noodles
Salt and freshly ground black pepper
2 tablespoons fresh chopped parsley
Yogurt

Heat the oil in a skillet until it is very hot, and add the meat.

Fry the meat quickly over high heat, turning all the pieces to be sure they are well browned.

Put in the onion and carrot and continue to cook on medium high heat for 5 minutes, stirring to keep the mixture from burning.

Remove the meat and vegetables to a large pot and pour in the water.

Bring to a boil and add the mung beans.

Partially cover the pot and simmer on low heat for about 40 minutes, until the beans open.

Add the potato, and cook, covered, on medium heat for 10 minutes. Add the noodles and cook for 5 more minutes.

Sprinkle with salt and pepper to taste and cook for another 5 minutes. Skim off any fat on the surface.

Ladle the soup into bowls and sprinkle each portion with parsley.

Place a dollop of yogurt in the center of each serving.

Serves 6.

With a green salad and/or omelet, flatbread or garlic bread, this soup can serve as a one-dish meal.

❧ BOUILLON WITH THIN NOODLES
(Khuil norin)

1 pound beef or lamb, cut into 1-inch cubes
8 cups beef or lamb broth
1⅓ cups cooked linguine
1 teaspoon butter
Salt
Freshly ground black pepper
1 small onion, peeled and diced
1 teaspoon cumin seeds

Put the meat and broth in a pot and bring to a boil. Reduce the heat and simmer over medium-low heat, partially covered, for 30 minutes.

Remove the meat with a slotted spoon and cut it into matchstick-size strips.

Return the meat to the pot.

Add the linguine, butter, salt and pepper to the pot and cook for another 20 minutes.

In a separate bowl, combine the onion and cumin with more black pepper to taste.

Ladle the soup into bowls and sprinkle each serving with some of the onion mixture.

Serves 6.

🦅 MEAT AND CABBAGE SOUP
(Karam shurva)

3 tablespoons vegetable oil
¾ pound lamb from shoulder, cut into ½-inch cubes
1 small onion, peeled and cut into thin semicircular rings
3 carrots, peeled and cut into rounds
2 cups crushed tomatoes
2 tablespoons tomato paste
½ small cabbage, coarsely shredded
6 cups water
1½ teaspoons cumin seeds, crushed
½ teaspoon hot paprika
Salt and pepper
2 potatoes, peeled and cut into ½-inch dice
2 tablespoons chopped fresh parsley

Heat the oil in a heavy pot or Dutch oven until it is very hot, and brown the lamb cubes on all sides over medium high heat.

Reduce the heat slightly, and add the onion and carrots, stirring as the vegetables soften.

Add the crushed tomatoes, tomato paste and cabbage, and cook over medium heat for 5 minutes.

Pour in the water, bring to a boil, and reduce the heat.

Add the cumin, paprika, and salt and pepper to taste.

Cover and simmer for 30 minutes.

Add the potatoes and cook for another 20 minutes.

Taste for seasoning, and just before serving, sprinkle with parsley.

Serves 6–8.

Accompanied by a cucumber and scallion salad and warm flatbread, this soup can serve as a one-dish meal.

🌿 TASHKENT BEEF AND CABBAGE SOUP
(Shchi)

(Adapted from *Taste the World with Seattle's Sister Cities*: Kearney, NE, Morris Press, 1989)

2 pounds brisket of beef
9 cups water
3 tablespoons butter
1 large onion, peeled and diced
½ medium head cabbage, shredded
1 can (28-ounces) tomatoes with juice, divided
2 tablespoons tomato paste
10 dried prunes, pitted
¼ cup golden raisins
1 tablespoon salt (or less, to taste)
1 tablespoon lemon juice
4 tablespoons brown sugar
2 tablespoons honey
2 tablespoons chopped fresh dill, divided
Sour cream

Remove any excess fat from the meat, put the meat and water in a large flameproof pot or Dutch oven, and bring to a boil.

Reduce the heat to medium and cook for 30 minutes. Skim off the foam.

Melt the butter and sauté the onion over medium-low heat for 3–5 minutes, until soft.

Add the cabbage, and sauté for 5 minutes.

Add half of the canned tomatoes with their juice, and cook for 10 minutes on medium low heat, stirring.

Put the cabbage mixture into the pot with the beef, and add the remaining tomatoes with their juice.

Stir in the tomato paste, prunes, raisins, salt, lemon juice, brown sugar, honey and 1 tablespoon of the dill.

Bring the soup to a boil, lower the heat, partially cover and simmer for 1 to 1¼ hours, until the meat is very tender.

Remove the meat from the heat and cut it into small (¾-inch) cubes.

Return the meat to the pot and heat the soup through.

Add the remaining tablespoon dill just before serving.

Serve with sour cream on the side.

Serves 8–10.

It is a good idea to let the soup chill overnight to allow the fat to congeal. Serve with flatbread and a salad for a one-dish meal, or with pumpkin or squash *samsas*.

🌿 MEAT AND TOMATO SOUP
(Pomidori shurva)

½ pound beef or lamb for stew
2 cloves garlic, peeled
2 medium carrots, peeled
1 medium potato, peeled
⅓ medium white radish (daikon), peeled (about ½ cup
    chopped white radish)
3 tablespoons vegetable oil
1 large onion, peeled and cut into semicircular rings
2½ cups water
2 cups tomato juice
⅓ cup sour cream
Salt and freshly ground black pepper

Chop the meat, garlic, carrots, potato and daikon coarsely.
Process them in a food processor for a few seconds until the
pieces are the size of small peas. Be careful not to overprocess into a purée.

Heat the oil in a heavy pot and sauté the onion until soft.

Add the meat and vegetables to the pot and cook, stirring,
over medium heat until the meat loses its pink color. Lower
the heat and cook for 6–8 minutes more, stirring to keep the
mixture from burning.

Add the water, bring the soup to a boil, and reduce the heat.
Simmer, partially covered, for 25 minutes.

Blend the tomato juice with the sour cream and stir it into
the soup. Cook for another 5 minutes. Be sure the mixture
is hot but do not allow it to boil.

Add salt and pepper to taste and allow the soup to simmer
for 5 more minutes.

Serves 6.

This soup has the consistency of a thin American cream soup; it is not as packed with ingredients as some of the other Uzbek meat soups, and makes a lighter starter for a meal.

✥ MEAT AND TURNIP SOUP
(Sholgom shurva)

8 cups strong beef or lamb broth
1 pound beef or lamb, cut into ½-inch cubes
2 medium turnips, peeled and diced
2 carrots, peeled and cut into 1-inch strips
1 small onion, peeled and cut into semicircular rings
½ small sweet red pepper, coarsely minced
2 tablespoons tomato paste
1 medium potato, peeled and cut into ½-inch cubes
Salt and freshly ground black pepper
Pinch cayenne pepper (optional)

Bring the meat broth to a boil and put in the meat, turnips, carrots, onion, and sweet red pepper.

Lower the heat, partially cover, and simmer 50 minutes.

Add the tomato paste and potato, and cook for 10–15 minutes.

Season with salt and the black pepper, and add the cayenne, if desired.

Serves 6.

❧ MEAT AND CHICKPEA SOUP
(*Mokhora*)

3 tablespoons vegetable oil
½ pound beef or lamb, cut into ¼-inch cubes or processed
    into pea-sized pieces in a food processor
1 small onion, peeled and cut into thin semicircular rings
3 medium carrots, peeled and diced
1½ cups crushed tomatoes
2 tablespoons tomato paste
6 cups water
Salt and pepper
2 medium potatoes, peeled and cut into ½-inch dice
1 cup cooked chickpeas
1 tablespoon chopped fresh parsley
2 tablespoons chopped fresh coriander

Heat the oil in a heavy pot or Dutch oven until it is very hot, and brown the meat on all sides over medium high heat.

Reduce the heat slightly and add the onion and carrots, stirring as the vegetables soften.

Add the crushed tomatoes and tomato paste, and cook over medium heat for 5 minutes.

Pour in the water, bring to a boil, and reduce the heat.

Add the salt and pepper to taste.

Cover and simmer for 30 minutes.

Add the potatoes and chickpeas, and cook for another 20 minutes.

Taste for seasoning, and just before serving sprinkle with parsley and coriander.

Serves 6–8.

A green salad and crisp flatbread go well with this dish.

🌺 MEAT AND NOODLE SOUP
(Suiuk osh)

3 tablespoons vegetable oil
1 medium onion, peeled and cut in semicircular rings
1½ pounds beef or lamb, cut in ½-inch cubes
1 carrot, peeled and cut in thin 1-inch long strips
1 garlic clove, peeled and diced
7 cups water
1 large potato, peeled and cut into ½-inch cubes
⅔ cup shredded cabbage
1 cup cooked angel-hair pasta
Salt and freshly ground black pepper to taste
Yogurt or sour cream

Heat the oil in a Dutch oven and put in the onion.

Cook for 2–3 minutes until the onion becomes translucent, and then add the meat, carrot, and garlic.

Cook over low heat, stirring, for 15 minutes.

Slowly pour in the water, raise the heat and bring the mixture to a boil.

Lower the heat, partially cover the pot, and cook slowly for 50 minutes.

Stir in the potato and cabbage and cook for 15 minutes.

Add the pasta to the pot and cook for 5 minutes, until the pasta is heated through.

Add salt and pepper to taste and simmer 5 minutes.

Can be served with yogurt or sour cream on the side.

Serves 6.

🦋 NOODLE, LAMB AND VEGETABLE SOUP
(Lagman)

(Adapted from Anya von Bremzen and John Welchman, *Please to the Table:* New York: Workman Publishing, 1990)

⅔ cup vegetable oil
1½ pounds boneless lamb shoulder or lamb for stew, cut into ½-inch cubes
3 small onions, peeled and finely chopped
3 carrots, peeled and diced
⅔ cup white radish (daikon), diced
2 small Italian or bell peppers, cored and diced
2 large potatoes, peeled and diced
1 (1-pound) can crushed tomatoes and juice
1 teaspoon powdered coriander
½ teaspoon ground cumin
2 large cloves garlic, peeled and crushed
Pinch cayenne pepper (optional)
1 bay leaf
Salt and freshly ground black pepper to taste
8 cups lamb or beef broth
2 teaspoons red wine vinegar
2 cups cooked flat egg noodles
¼ cup chopped fresh parsley
¼ cup chopped fresh coriander

Heat the oil and brown the lamb on all sides until it loses its pink color.

Remove the meat to a separate plate.

Brown the onions, carrots, daikon, and peppers for 10–15 minutes, and add the potatoes.

Simmer the mixture for another 5 minutes, taking care that the potatoes do not burn, and adding more oil if necessary.

Add the tomatoes and stir well.

Stir in the powdered coriander, cumin, 1 clove of the garlic, the cayenne if you are using it, and the bay leaf.

Sprinkle with salt and pepper, and add the meat.

Pour in the stock and bring the mixture to a boil over medium high heat, stirring to keep the meat and vegetables from burning.

Simmer, covered, for about 50 minutes.

Add the remaining clove of garlic and the vinegar, and taste for seasoning, adding more vinegar and salt and pepper as needed.

Put in the noodles and simmer for a few minutes until the pasta is heated through.

Ladle into bowls, being sure that each portion receives some of the noodles.

Mix the parsley and coriander, and sprinkle some over each plate of soup.

Serves 6.

This soup is always served with flatbread. With a green salad or a cucumber salad it can serve as a one-dish meal.

🦁 LAMB, CARROT AND NOODLE SOUP
(Lagman 2)

(Adapted from the Uzbekistan Tandoori Bread Bakery, Kew Gardens, New York, courtesy of Isak Barayev)

2 tablespoons vegetable oil
1 pound lamb or beef for stew, cut into ½-inch cubes
3 medium onions, peeled and diced
1 sweet red pepper, seeded, ribbed and diced
4 celery stems, diced
3 medium cloves garlic, peeled and finely minced
8 cups water
2 large carrots, peeled and diced
1 cup fresh or canned tomatoes, peeled, seeded
    and chopped
1 tablespoon tomato paste
½ teaspoon ground cumin
¼ teaspoon hot paprika
¼ teaspoon cayenne pepper, or to taste
Salt and freshly ground black pepper
¼ cup chopped fresh coriander
¼ cup chopped fresh dill
½ pound (3 cups) hot cooked spaghetti or flat egg noodles

In a heavy pot heat the oil and add the meat, stirring to brown well.

Remove the meat with a slotted spoon to a plate.

Put the onions in the pot and sauté them until they are very soft, about 8–10 minutes.

Add the red pepper, celery, and garlic, and cook over low heat for 10–12 minutes.

Pour in the water, and add the carrots, tomatoes, tomato paste, cumin, paprika, cayenne and salt and black pepper to taste.

Simmer, covered, for 25 minutes. Skim off any fat from the surface.

Sprinkle in the coriander and dill.

Place about ½ cup of the hot pasta in each of 6 large soup bowls. Ladle the soup over the pasta.

Serves 6.

Lagman should be served with flatbread.

☙ LAMB AND VEGETABLE SOUP
(Shurpa)

(Courtesy of Boris Elyukin and Elena Granovsky)

¼ cup corn oil
1 pound meaty lamb bones
½ pound lamb, cut into 1-inch cubes
1 large carrot, peeled and coarsely sliced
1 stick celery, coarsely chopped
½ sweet red pepper, cut into ½-inch pieces
¾ teaspoon salt
½ teaspoon freshly ground black pepper
1 teaspoon cumin seeds, crushed with a rolling pin
1 teaspoon tomato paste
5 cups water
1 medium potato, peeled and cut into eighths
1 (8-ounces) can chickpeas, drained
1 stick celery, coarsely chopped
½ cup chopped fresh dill
¼ cup chopped fresh flat-leaf parsley
2 scallions, green parts only, minced

In a heavy pot heat the oil over medium high until it is barely smoking, and add the lamb bones. Cook for 7–8 minutes on medium high heat, stirring to brown the lamb on all sides.

Add the meat cubes and cook for another 5 minutes to brown the meat.

Lower the heat to medium, and put in the carrots, celery, red pepper, salt, black pepper, cumin and tomato paste. Stir over medium heat for 4–5 minutes.

Add the water, stir to blend the ingredients, and simmer over medium-low heat, partially covered, for 35 minutes.

Stir in the potato and chickpeas, and cook for another 15 minutes.

Remove the lamb bones, and sprinkle in half of the dill, parsley and scallions.

Ladle the soup into bowls, and sprinkle each serving with the remaining dill, parsley and scallions.

Serves 6.

❦ LAMB AND BEAN SOUP
(Lovia oshi)

3 tablespoons vegetable oil
1 medium onion, peeled and diced
¾ pound beef or lamb, cut into ½-inch cubes
1 carrot, peeled and cut into ½-inch cubes
2 medium tomatoes, diced
2 tablespoons tomato paste
7 cups water
1½ cups cooked white beans
Salt and freshly ground black pepper
1 tablespoon chopped fresh parsley

Heat the oil in a Dutch oven and sauté the onion until it starts to color, about 5 minutes.

Add the meat and stir until browned.

On low heat add the carrot, tomatoes and tomato paste, and stir.

Slowly pour in the water, stirring constantly to blend all the ingredients. Raise the heat and bring the soup to a boil.

Lower the heat, partially cover and cook for 45 minutes.

Add the beans and salt and pepper to taste, and cook for another 20 minutes.

Sprinkle in the parsley just before serving.

Serves 6.

❧ LAMB AND APPLE SOUP
(Kavirma shurpa)

2 tablespoons vegetable oil
½ pound lamb, cut into ¼ to ½-inch cubes
1 small onion, peeled and cut into semicircular rings
2 tomatoes, trimmed and cut into ½-inch chunks
2 tablespoons tomato paste
3 tablespoons chopped fresh coriander, divided
2 tablespoons chopped fresh dill
2 tablespoons chopped fresh parsley
Pinch cayenne pepper
6 cups water
2 medium potatoes, peeled and cut into ½-inch cubes
1 large tart apple, peeled, cored and cut into ½-inch cubes
Salt and freshly ground black pepper

Heat the oil in a Dutch oven or heavy pot and sauté the lamb on medium-high heat until well browned.

Add the onion and cook for 2–3 minutes until it softens.

Put in the tomatoes, tomato paste, 2 tablespoons of the coriander, the dill, parsley and cayenne pepper.

Lower the heat to medium and cook for 7–8 minutes, stirring to keep the mixture from burning.

Pour in the water and bring to a boil.

Stir in the potatoes and apple, and add salt and pepper to taste.

Cover the pot and cook on low heat for 35 minutes.

Taste for seasoning, and add salt and pepper as needed.

Just before serving, sprinkle with the remaining tablespoon of coriander.

Serves 6.

Serve with flatbread on the side or with crisp flatbread croutons.

🌿 SOUP WITH MEATBALLS
(Kifta shurva)

FOR THE MEATBALLS
¾ pound ground beef or lamb
½ small onion, peeled and finely diced
1 raw egg white
⅓ cup cooked rice
Salt
Freshly ground black pepper

FOR THE SOUP
5 cups beef broth
1 large carrot, peeled and coarsely chopped
1 large potato, peeled and coarsely chopped
1 can (15 ounces) crushed tomatoes
1 cup drained cooked chickpeas
¼ teaspoon ground cumin
¼ teaspoon sweet paprika
¼ teaspoon freshly ground black pepper
2 tablespoons chopped fresh parsley, divided
2 tablespoons chopped fresh coriander, divided
Yogurt (optional)

Combine the ground meat, onion, egg white, rice and salt and form into long meatball kebabs about 2 to 2½ inches in length and ¾-inch wide, tapering towards the ends.

Put the broth in a Dutch oven or large flame-proof casserole and add the carrot, potatoes, tomatoes, chickpeas, cumin, paprika, pepper, 1 tablespoon parsley and 1 tablespoon coriander.

Bring the soup to a boil, reduce the heat slightly, and carefully add the meatballs.

Stir gently, being careful not to break up the meat.

Cover and cook over medium low heat for 20–25 minutes.

Ladle the soup into serving bowls and sprinkle each portion with the remaining parsley and coriander.

Serves 6–8.

While this soup is not served with yogurt in Uzbekistan, Russians often add a dollop to each plate with very positive results!

SOUP WITH MEATBALLS AND CHICKPEAS
(Mastava)

½ pound ground beef or lamb
2 small onions, peeled and minced (divided)
Salt and freshly ground black pepper
Flour for dusting (about ¼ cup)
8 cups beef or lamb broth
1 cup cooked chickpeas
2 large carrots, peeled and diced
3 tablespoons tomato paste
½ small red bell pepper, seeded and ribs removed, cut
    into thin 1-inch long strips
Pinch cayenne pepper
1 large potato, peeled and diced
¾ cup rice
¼ cup chopped fresh coriander, + 1 tablespoon for garnish
Yogurt

Mix the ground meat with 1 of the minced onions, and add salt and pepper to taste. This soup is spicy, so be generous with the pepper!

Form into tiny meatballs the size of cherries.

Dust the meatballs lightly with flour.

Bring the broth to a boil, reduce the heat to medium, and carefully lower in the meatballs.

Add the chickpeas, carrots, remaining onion, tomato paste, bell pepper and cayenne.

Simmer, partially covered, on medium heat for 15 minutes.

Add the potato and sprinkle in the rice.

Partially cover the pot and cook for another 20 minutes.

Taste for seasoning, and add salt and pepper as needed. Add the ¼ cup coriander.

Ladle the soup into bowls, sprinkle each with a bit more coriander, and serve with yogurt on the side.

Serves 6–8.

With a green salad and flatbread, this soup makes a good one-dish meal. Fresh fruit or ice cream go well for dessert.

🌿 SOUP WITH PELMENI
(*Chuchvara shurva*)

2 tablespoons vegetable oil
1 small onion, peeled and finely chopped
3 tablespoons tomato paste
8 cups beef or lamb broth
32 *chuchvara*, uncooked (see recipe, p. 174)
Salt and pepper

Heat the oil and fry the onion on medium high heat until golden brown, about 5–7 minutes.

Add the tomato paste and stir well.

Slowly pour in the meat broth, mixing well.

Bring the soup to a boil and drop in the *chuchvara*.

Simmer for 5–7 minutes until the dumplings rise to the surface.

Add salt and pepper to taste.

Serves 4–6.

The soup can be served with sour cream on the side.

🦎 CHICKEN AND SPINACH SOUP
(Shovul shurva)

8 cups water
1 pound chicken thighs, legs, or breasts
1 small onion, peeled and cut in thin semicircular rings
3 medium potatoes, peeled and diced
1 package (10 ounces) frozen spinach or 2 cups fresh
    spinach leaves, washed and coarsely chopped
Salt and freshly ground black pepper
2 eggs

Bring the water and chicken pieces to a boil and simmer, partially covered, for 30 minutes.

Remove the chicken pieces with a slotted spoon, discard the bones and skin, dice the chicken meat, and return it to the pot.

Add the onion, potatoes, and spinach, and simmer for 20 minutes.

Sprinkle with salt and pepper to taste.

Beat the eggs well in a small bowl, and slowly pour them into the pot, stirring constantly.

Simmer for 5 minutes, taste for seasoning, and serve very hot.

Serves 8.

Meat *samsas* make a good accompaniment to this soup.

🦃 CHICKEN AND EGG SOUP
(Tovuk yushak)

4 tablespoons vegetable oil
2 medium carrots, peeled and diced
2 small onions, peeled and diced
1 stalk celery, diced
2 chicken breasts, skinned and boned, cut into
    1-inch cubes
7 cups water
2 large potatoes, peeled and diced
¼ teaspoon powdered coriander
⅛ teaspoon powdered cumin
Salt and freshly ground black pepper
2 eggs, well beaten
¼ cup chopped fresh parsley
¼ cup chopped fresh coriander

In a large heavy pot or Dutch oven heat the oil and stir in the carrots, onions and celery.

Cook over medium heat, stirring, for 2–3 minutes, and add the chicken meat.

Cook, stirring, for another 5 minutes.

Pour in the water, bring to a boil, and reduce the heat. Simmer the pot, partially covered, for 35 minutes.

Add the potatoes, powdered coriander, cumin, salt and pepper, and simmer for another 20 minutes.

Raise the heat slightly and pour in the eggs, whisking constantly until the egg forms thin threads. Stir in the parsley and coriander, and serve. (Note: do not continue cooking after the egg threads are formed because they will become tough).

Serves 8.

🦎 CHICKEN SOUP WITH NOODLES
(Tovuk gushtli ugra oshi)

10 cups water
1 chicken (4 pounds), skin removed and cut into
    serving pieces
1 large onion, peeled and cut into julienne
3 medium carrots, cut into julienne
Salt and pepper
2 medium potatoes, peeled and cut into julienne
1 cup thin egg noodles

Place the water, chicken and onion in a large pot and bring to a boil. Lower the heat, partially cover, and simmer for 20–35 minutes.

Add the carrots and cook for 10 more minutes. Add salt and pepper to taste.

Bring to a boil, add the potatoes and noodles, and lower the heat to a simmer.

Cook for another 10–15 minutes, until the noodles and potatoes are cooked through.

Check for seasoning and add salt and pepper as needed.

Serves 6–8.

Serve with a flatbread or with French garlic bread.

🌿 FISH SOUP
(Shurbomokhi)

1 pound fish fillets such as cod or halibut, cut into
    1½-inch pieces
Salt
7 cups water
1 medium onion, peeled and quartered
2 carrots, peeled and coarsely chopped
2 medium potatoes, peeled and coarsely chopped
1 bay leaf
2 cloves garlic, peeled
2 tablespoons fresh chopped coriander

Sprinkle the pieces of fish lightly with salt and set aside for 10 minutes. Rinse them under running water.

Bring the water to a boil and add the onion, carrots and potatoes.

Reduce the heat and simmer at medium heat for 15 minutes. Remove the onion.

Add the fish and the bay leaf, and simmer for 8–10 minutes. Do not overcook.

Crush the garlic, and mix with ½ teaspoon salt, blending well. You can use a small mortar and pestle or put the mixture through a garlic press.

Add the garlic and salt to the soup and simmer 2 minutes. Remove the bay leaf.

Sprinkle with coriander just before serving.

Serves 6.

Serve with crisp rye crackers or flatbread.

🌿 BEET AND TURNIP SOUP
(Oshi sholgom kizilcha)

7 cups chicken broth or 5 cups water and 4 chicken
    bouillon cubes
2 cans (1 pound each) beets, diced, with their liquid
4 turnips, peeled and diced
1 small onion, diced
4 carrots, peeled and diced
2 pounds skinless chicken breast, cut into ½-inch cubes
¾ teaspoon ground cumin
Salt and pepper
2 tablespoons chopped fresh parsley

Bring the chicken broth to a boil and stir in the beets with
their liquid, turnips, onion, carrots, chicken, and cumin.

Sprinkle with salt and pepper to taste, but be careful with
the salt, as the amount needed will depend on the salt content of the chicken broth.

Partially cover the pot and simmer the soup for 45 minutes
to 1 hour, until the chicken is done and the soup is flavorful.

Taste for seasoning and add salt and pepper as needed. Just
before serving sprinkle in the parsley.

Serves 8.

This soup can be served with pumpkin or mushroom *samsas*,
or with an Uzbek flatbread.

🌿 RICE AND TURNIP SOUP
(Katikli sholgum khurda)

7 cups water
1 small onion, finely chopped
2 medium turnips, peeled and diced in ½-inch cubes
3 large carrots, peeled and sliced in ¼-inch rounds
2 medium potatoes, peeled and cut into ½-inch cubes
1 cup rice
1 teaspoon salt
¼ teaspoon ground black pepper
Pinch cayenne pepper (optional)
Yogurt
2 tablespoons chopped parsley

Bring the water to a boil and add onion, turnips, and carrots. Simmer for 5–10 minutes.

Pour in the potatoes, rice, salt, black pepper and optional cayenne.

Stir and bring the mixture back to a boil.

Lower the heat, cover, and simmer for 20–25 minutes until the potatoes and rice are thoroughly cooked and the soup has thickened slightly.

Taste for seasoning and add salt and pepper as needed.

Ladle the soup into bowls and place a heaping tablespoonful of yogurt in the center of each dish.

Sprinkle with the parsley and serve immediately.

Serves 6.

Meat *samsas* make a good accompaniment to this soup. It can also be served with a tomato salad and flatbread.

❧ MUSHROOM AND RICE SOUP
(Kuizikorin shurva)

10 ounces mushrooms, washed and coarsely chopped
6 cups chicken broth
1 cup cooked rice
Salt
1 tablespoon butter (optional)
2 eggs, well beaten
1½ tablespoons chopped fresh dill

Parboil the mushrooms for 3 minutes. Drain well.

Heat the chicken broth and add the rice.

Add salt to taste. How much salt is needed will depend on the saltiness of the chicken broth.

If you are using the butter, add it to the soup and stir until it melts.

Keep the soup simmering, and slowly pour in the eggs, whisking constantly.

Ladle the soup into bowls and sprinkle each serving with some of the dill.

Serves 6.

This is good with crisp flatbread and with meat or squash *samsas.*

🌿 PUMPKIN-RICE MILK SOUP
(Shirkovok)

4 cups water
Salt to taste
⅔ cup rice
1½ cups diced pumpkin meat, or 1½ cups diced
    yellow zucchini
4 cups milk (do not use skim milk)
1 tablespoon butter or margarine
Sour cream

Put the water in a pot, add the salt, and bring to a boil.

Add the rice and the pumpkin or zucchini, reduce the heat, cover, and cook for 20 minutes on low heat.

Reserve 1 cup of the cooking liquid from the rice mixture, and pour off the rest.

Stir together the rice, pumpkin and 1 cup of the reserved liquid, and add the milk.

Raise the heat to medium and cook for a few minutes until the soup is heated through, but do not boil.

Add salt to taste.

Put in 1 tablespoon butter or margarine, and stir until melted.

Serve with sour cream on the side.

Serves 6.

This soup is usually served with a crisp flatbread. It goes well before a chicken main course or *shashlyk*.

❧ MUNG BEAN AND PUMPKIN SOUP
(Mash kovok)

1 small onion, peeled and diced
1 tablespoon butter
7 cups water
¾ cup mung beans, washed and picked over
1 cup cooked white beans
2 medium potatoes, peeled and diced
2 cups pumpkin or 2 medium yellow zucchini,
    coarsely chopped
Salt and freshly ground black pepper
1 tablespoon chopped fresh parsley
1 tablespoon chopped fresh basil
Sour cream

Sauté the onion in the butter in a small skillet until golden.

Place the water in a large flameproof pot and add the onion.

Put in the mung beans and bring to a boil. Lower the heat to medium, partially cover the pot, and cook for 30 minutes if the beans have not been presoaked and 10 minutes if they have been presoaked.

Add the white beans, potatoes and pumpkin or squash, and cook for 20 minutes. Season with salt and pepper to taste, and sprinkle in the parsley and basil. Serve with sour cream on the side.

Serves 6.

This soup is good with flatbreads and with meat *samsas*.

❧ CAULIFLOWER SOUP
(Gulkaram shurva)

9 cups water
¾ pound beef (soup shank or stew beef is fine)
1 onion, peeled and quartered
1 pound cauliflower (about 4 cups of florets from a fresh
    cauliflower, or a 1-pound package frozen cauliflower)
2 large carrots, peeled and diced
3 medium potatoes, peeled and diced
Salt and cayenne pepper to taste
2 tablespoons chopped fresh coriander

Bring the water and beef to a boil in a heavy pot, and add the onion. Lower the heat and simmer for 35 minutes.

Remove and discard the onion, cut the beef into bite-size pieces and return the meat to the pot.

Add the cauliflower, carrots, potatoes, and salt and cayenne to taste, partially cover the pot and simmer for 20 minutes.

Mash the cauliflower florets against the sides of the pot to make the pieces smaller.

Skim the fat from the soup (if you have time, chill it first).

Taste for seasoning, and sprinkle with the coriander just before serving.

Serves 6.

The soup can be served with a radish or cucumber salad, or with meat *samsas*.

❧ COLD MEAT AND YOGURT SOUP
(Yakhna katik)

2 cups buttermilk
1 cup yogurt
1 cup sour cream
1 cup ice water
½ pound cooked beef or lamb, cut into thin 1-inch
    long strips
4 Kirby cucumbers, peeled and diced
3 scallions, diced (green and white parts)
2 hard-boiled eggs, peeled and chopped
2 tablespoons chopped fresh Italian flatleaf parsley
2 tablespoons chopped fresh dill
2 tablespoons chopped fresh coriander
Salt

In a large bowl combine the buttermilk, yogurt, sour cream and water, and mix well.

Add all the other ingredients, and chill for at least 3 hours.

Check for seasoning before serving, and add salt or herbs as needed.

Serves 6.

This soup is good in summer with a chicken salad or with a tomato and lettuce salad.

❧ COLD SOUR MILK AND HERB SOUP
(Chalop)

2 cups buttermilk
1 cup yogurt
1 cup sour cream
1 cup water
6 Kirby cucumbers, peeled, seeded and diced
10 red radishes, diced
½ cup diced white radish (daikon)
4 scallions, diced (green and white parts)
2 tablespoons chopped fresh parsley
2 tablespoons chopped fresh dill
2 tablespoons chopped fresh coriander
Salt and freshly ground black pepper

In a large bowl stir the buttermilk, yogurt, sour cream and water until smooth.

Add the diced cucumbers, radishes, daikon and scallions, and stir until smooth.

Sprinkle in the herbs and salt and pepper to taste.

Chill for at least 3 hours.

Serves 6.

The soup can be served with very crisp thin flatbread or whole-wheat crackers.

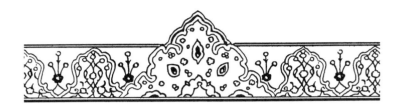

MEATS,
POULTRY AND
FISH

By far the most popular meat in Uzbekistan, lamb is the major ingredient in *plov*, grilled kebabs (*shashlyk*), meatballs and stews. Baked, grilled, roasted and braised, lamb is a favorite filling for various kinds of dumplings and meat pies. Cut in tiny chunks or ground, the meat is mixed with diced onions, dill, coriander, pepper and salt, marinated for several hours in a variety of liquids and spices, including pomegranate and lemon juice, vinegar, and sparkling water, and grilled on skewers. Quartered tomatoes, pomegranates and an assortment of vegetable salads accompany the kebabs.

The piece of lamb fat that makes up the tail of a fat-tailed sheep, *kurdiuk*, is a prized staple of Uzbek cooking. The fat, which does not fully melt when rendered, leaves a residue of tiny crackling grains, a delicacy included in the resulting stew or *plov*. In light of American dietary habits and of the lack of fat-tailed sheep, however, recipes with *kurdiuk*, *khasyp* (a home-made sausage with subproducts such as hearts and lungs), and recipes using horsemeat have been omitted.

Beef, lamb, chicken, and beef and lamb liver are the most common ingredients in these Uzbek meat recipes. The majority of the dishes can be made with either beef or lamb; Uzbek cookbooks, in fact, often call for "meat" without specifying which of the two should be used. Since the country is predominantly Muslim, pork and pork products are not part of the national cuisine. Meat dishes include grilled kebabs and many recipes call for slow braising, stewing and steaming. Some stews make heavier use of vegetables than of meat and are quite low in fat, since the ingredients are stewed in their own juice without any additional lard or oil. It is always a good idea, however, to skim the fat from the top of any stew or casserole dish.

The size of the pieces of meat used in these dishes varies. In some cases fairly large cubes of meat are needed, while in others the meat should be cut into ¼-inch cubes. While you can use a food processor to reduce the meat to such tiny pea-sized pieces, be careful not to overprocess the beef or lamb into a mass of ground meat.

For grilling *shashlyks* flat skewers are preferable to round ones, because the cubes of meat are less likely to slide off them; ground meat in particular tends to fall off round skewers. When using wooden skewers be sure to soak them for at least 10 minutes in water before using to keep them from burning during the grilling process.

Though lamb and beef are more common than fowl, Uzbek chicken dishes include grilled chicken, chicken kebabs, chicken with pasta, and chicken slowly stewed with vegetables. In most of these recipes Cornish hen can be substituted for chicken.

Since isolated mountain lakes and streams are the only sources of fish, which is virtually unavailable in the flat, desert areas of the country, it does not play an important role in Uzbek cuisine. Fried fish, however, a specialty of the Bukharan Jews, is found in ordinary Uzbek recipes, served both as an appetizer and as a main course.

MEAT

❧ LAMB KEBABS (SHASHLYK) 1
(Sikh kebab)

3 pounds lamb, cut from the leg into 1½-inch cubes
6 tablespoons fresh lemon juice
2 medium onions, minced
3 tablespoons finely chopped coriander
1 tablespoon ground coriander
3 cloves garlic, minced
1 teaspoon salt

FOR GARNISH
Tomatoes
Onions
Chopped parsley

Combine all the ingredients except the lamb in a glass bowl and stir well.

Add the lamb cubes and toss well.

Allow the mixture to chill in the refrigerator overnight (at least 12 hours), stirring occasionally.

Drain off the marinade.

Sprinkle the meat lightly with salt, and thread the pieces onto metal skewers. Do not crowd them; the pieces should not touch each other.

Grill or broil the lamb at least 4 inches from the flame, from 7–12 minutes, depending on how rare or well done you like the meat.

Serves 6.

Serve with tomatoes and onions sprinkled with chopped parsley.

⅗ LAMB KEBABS (SHASHLYK) 2
(Sikh kebab)

2 pounds lamb, fat removed, cut into very small
    (½-inch) cubes
Salt
Freshly ground black pepper
1 teaspoon cumin seeds, crushed
1 teaspoon sweet paprika
Pinch cayenne pepper (optional)
Seltzer water
2 large white onions, peeled (divided)

Sprinkle the lamb cubes with the salt, pepper, cumin and paprika, and the cayenne, if you are using it.

Mince one of the onions and add it to the mixture,

Place the cubes in a single layer in a glass or enamel dish and pour in enough seltzer water to barely cover them.

Place a weight on the pan (a large plate with cans on top of it will do) and allow the dish with the meat to marinate in the refrigerator for at least 2–3 hours, or overnight if you have the time.

Drain off the marinade, pat the meat dry, and thread the pieces on skewers. (If you are using wooden skewers, be sure to soak them for at least 10 minutes in water to keep them from burning).

Grill over hot coals, on an electric grill or under a broiler for 5–7 minutes on each side, depending on how rare you like the meat. The cubes should be browned on the outside and slightly pink on the inside.

Slice the remaining onion into thin rings and serve with the meat.

Serves 4.

Serve with a garnish of fresh tomatoes, pomegranate seeds and a pitcher of white spiced vinegar.

Variation: Replace the seltzer water with either tomato juice or pomegranate juice.

❈ LAMB KEBABS (SHASHLYK) 3
(Sikh kebab)

(Adapted from *Taste the World with Seattle's Sister Cities*: Morris Press, NE, 1989)

2 pounds lamb, cut into 1½-inch cubes
1 medium onion, peeled and chopped
2 tablespoons cumin seeds, crushed
1 teaspoon salt
¼ teaspoon freshly ground black pepper
1 cup dry white wine
½ cup vegetable oil

Put the lamb cubes into a glass bowl.

Combine the onion, cumin seeds, salt, pepper, white wine, and oil.

Pour the marinade over the lamb cubes and add enough water to just cover the meat.

Marinate for at least 8 hours or overnight in the refrigerator.

Drain off the marinade and thread the meat onto skewers.

Do not crowd them; the pieces should not touch each other.

Grill the lamb over hot coals or in the broiler, from 10–14 minutes, depending on how rare you like the meat.

Serves 4.

Serve with tomatoes and onions sprinkled with chopped parsley.

❧ MEAT SHASHLYK
(Titrama Kebab)

This dish can be prepared as a *shashlyk* on skewers or as ground meat cutlets.

1½ pounds beef or lamb, either cut in 2-inch cubes,
    or ground
½ teaspoon salt
½ teaspoon freshly ground black pepper
½ teaspoon cumin seeds, crushed
½ teaspoon powdered coriander
1 tablespoon chopped fresh basil
1 tablespoon chopped fresh Italian flat-leaf parsley
1 tablespoon chopped fresh dill
½ medium onion, peeled
1 clove garlic, peeled
1 medium tomato

In a small bowl combine the salt, pepper, cumin seeds, coriander, basil, parsley, and dill.

FOR MEAT CUBES:
Place the meat cubes in a glass bowl and sprinkle with the spice mixture.

96

FOR GROUND MEAT:
Combine the ground meat with the spices and mix well.

FOR BOTH:
Put the onion, garlic and tomato through a food processor.

FOR MEAT CUBES:
Pour the vegetable mixture over the meat.

FOR GROUND MEAT:
Combine the ground meat thoroughly with this mixture, blending with your hands until a solid mass is formed.

FOR BOTH:
Put the bowl with the meat in the refrigerator to chill for at least 1 hour.

FOR THE MEAT CUBES:
Thread the meat onto skewers and cook over a grill or in the broiler until meat is done. Serve with fresh tomato and cucumber slices.

FOR THE GROUND MEAT:
Form into "sausages" 3 inches long and 1 inch wide, tapering them at the ends. Broil for about 5–8 minutes on each side.

On skewers: Serves 3.
Ground cutlets: Makes about 15 cutlets.

Serve with rice.

🦂 LAMB AND VEGETABLE STEW
(Oshi mash)

1 pound lamb for stew
4 tablespoons vegetable oil
1 medium onion, cut in semicircular rings
1½ cups mung beans, picked over
2 medium turnips, peeled and coarsely chopped
2 large carrots, peeled and coarsely chopped
1¼ cups shredded cabbage
1¾ cups rice
1 teaspoon cumin seeds, crushed
½ teaspoon ground cumin
½ teaspoon sweet paprika
Salt and freshly ground black pepper
9 cups water

Put the lamb through the food processor until the pieces are the size of peas, but do not grind it into a mass that sticks together.

Heat the oil in a large flame-proof Dutch oven or casserole, and sauté the lamb and onion over medium heat for a few minutes, until the onions are soft and the meat is lightly browned.

On very low heat add the mung beans, turnips, carrots, cabbage, rice, cumin seeds and ground cumin, paprika, salt and pepper, and stir well. Pour in the water and cover the casserole.

Cook on low heat for at least 1 hour, until the mixture is very soft. Check occasionally to be sure there is enough water and that the stew does not burn.

Serves 8.

Serve with crisp flatbread and a cucumber salad.

❧ LAMB AND VEGETABLES
(Zharkop)

⅓ cup vegetable oil
2½ pounds boneless lamb shoulder, cut into 1-inch cubes
2 medium onions, peeled and coarsely chopped
3 carrots, coarsely chopped
2 Italian pale green peppers or 1 green bell pepper,
    cored, seeded and cut into thin strips (do not use
    hot peppers)
¼ cup tomato paste
Salt
½ teaspoon freshly ground black pepper
Pinch cayenne pepper
¾ teaspoon cumin seeds
½ teaspoon powdered coriander
1 cup beef broth
4 large potatoes, peeled and diced
2 cloves garlic, peeled and minced
½ cup chopped fresh coriander
⅓ cup chopped fresh parsley
2 pita or *non* breads, toasted and quartered

Heat the oil in a heavy pot or large Dutch oven.

Brown the lamb on all sides, stirring constantly.

Remove the lamb with a slotted spoon, and add the onions, carrots and peppers to the pot. Sauté the vegetables, stirring, for about 10 minutes. Pour off most of the fat.

Return the lamb to the pot and mix in the tomato paste, salt, black pepper, cayenne, cumin seeds, powdered coriander, and the beef broth.

Lower the heat, cover the pot and simmer until the meat is tender, for about 1 hour.

Add the potatoes and garlic, and cook for 15 minutes.

Stir in half of the coriander and parsley and the pieces of bread, and simmer for 1 or 2 minutes.

Sprinkle with the remaining fresh herbs just before serving.

Serves 4–5.

🦁 BAKED LAMB STEW SAMARKAND
(Dimlama Samarkand)

1 pound lamb for stew, cut into 1-inch cubes
Salt
1 small onion, peeled and cut into rings
2 large carrots, peeled and coarsely sliced
2 medium potatoes, peeled and cut into 1-inch cubes
1 small sweet Italian pepper, peeled, ribs removed and
    cut into 1-inch pieces
1 large clove garlic, peeled and crushed
1 can (15 ounces) crushed tomatoes
¾ cup water
1 tablespoon chopped fresh dill
2 tablespoons chopped fresh coriander
2 tablespoons chopped fresh parsley

Preheat the oven to 350 degrees.

Place the lamb cubes in an oven-proof casserole large enough to hold all the ingredients, and sprinkle the meat lightly with salt.

Add all the other ingredients and stir just to blend.

Bake for 45–55 minutes, until meat is very tender.

Serves 4.

This dish is good served over noodles or rice, and accompanied by a radish or cucumber salad.

❧ LAMB STEW
(Dimlama)

(Adapted from *Taste the World with Seattle's Sister Cities*: Morris Press, NE, 1989)

½ small head of cabbage
1½ pounds lamb, cut into 1-inch cubes
2 large potatoes, peeled and cut into 1-inch cubes
Salt to taste
1½ teaspoons cumin seeds, crushed (divided)
1 sweet Italian green pepper, coarsely chopped
1 medium onion, peeled and cut into semicircular rings
1 can (8 ounces) crushed tomatoes, with juice
1 cup lamb or chicken broth

Remove 4 large leaves from the cabbage and wash them well.

Wash the remaining cabbage, and chop coarsely.

Line a large flame-proof casserole or Dutch oven with the 4 big cabbage leaves.

Cover the leaves with the lamb and potatoes, and sprinkle them with salt to taste and with ½ teaspoon of the cumin.

Layer the green peppers and onions on top of the lamb and potatoes, and sprinkle with more salt and ½ teaspoon cumin.

Crush the tomatoes. Place the cabbage and the crushed tomatoes with their juice on top of the peppers and onions. Sprinkle with salt and the remaining cumin.

Pour the broth over the casserole and bring to a boil.

Reduce the heat, cover and simmer for 1 hour, or until the meat is very tender.

Serves 4–5.

🌿 LAMB WITH CHICKPEAS
(Guisht nukhot)

6 tablespoons butter
2 pounds lamb from neck or leg, cut into ½-inch cubes
1 can (1 pound) chickpeas, drained
½ cup lamb or beef broth
3 tomatoes, peeled and coarsely chopped
2 tablespoons tomato paste
Salt and pepper
¼ cup chopped fresh parsley

Melt the butter in a Dutch oven or heavy casserole and sauté the lamb until it is well browned.

Add the chickpeas and cook, stirring, for another 5 minutes.

Stir in the broth, tomatoes, and tomato paste, and season with salt and pepper to taste.

Cover the casserole and simmer over low heat for 30 minutes, or until the meat is very tender.

Taste for seasoning, and sprinkle with the parsley just before serving.

Serves 4.

❧ LAMB AND STRING BEANS
(*Guisht lovia*)

3 tablespoons butter
1 large onion, finely chopped
2 pounds beef for stew, cut in ½-inch cubes
2 cups string beans, fresh, frozen or canned
3 tablespoons tomato paste
1 cup beef broth
2 cloves garlic, crushed
5 black peppercorns, crushed
Salt to taste
1 tablespoon chopped fresh basil
1 tablespoon chopped fresh coriander
2 tablespoons chopped fresh parsley, divided

Melt the butter in a heavy casserole or Dutch oven, and sauté the onion until it is soft and golden but not brown.

Add the meat and cook over medium high heat, stirring, until the meat is well browned.

If you are using fresh or frozen string beans cook them briefly in boiling salted water until they start to soften; if you are using canned beans, drain them well.

Stir the beans, tomato paste, beef broth and crushed garlic into the meat and onions, and add the peppercorns and salt to taste.

Sprinkle in the basil, coriander, and 1 tablespoon of the parsley.

Blend the mixture well, cover and simmer on low heat for 30–35 minutes, until the meat is thoroughly cooked.

Just before serving sprinkle with the additional tablespoon of parsley.

Serves 4.

Serve over rice or noodles.

🌿 LAMB AND EGGS
(Kovurma nukus)

4 tablespoons vegetable oil
1½ pounds lamb from neck or shoulder, cut into thin
    strips (approximately 2 inches long × ½-inch wide)
1 medium onion, cut into thin semicircular rings
1 can (1 pound) crushed tomatoes, with juice
Salt and pepper
1 large clove garlic, peeled and crushed
1 tablespoon chopped fresh coriander
2 tablespoons chopped fresh parsley, divided
1 egg
1 teaspoon water
1 teaspoon butter

Heat the oil and sauté the lamb until lightly browned.

Stir in the onion, and cook until soft.

Add the tomatoes and salt and pepper to taste, cover, and simmer on low heat for 25–30 minutes, until lamb is thoroughly cooked.

Add the garlic, coriander, and one tablespoon of the parsley.

Beat the egg and water together with a fork to blend well.

In a small pan melt the butter and pour in the egg mixture.

Cook to form a small dry omelet, turning once.

Cut the omelet into thin (approximately 2 inches long by ¼-inch wide) strips, and stir into the meat mixture.

Sprinkle with the remaining parsley and serve.

Serves 3–4.

This dish can be served with fried potatoes or over rice.

❦ GROUND LAMB KEBAB
(Kijma kebab)

2 pounds ground lamb
1 medium onion, very finely chopped
1 teaspoon cumin seed, crushed
1 teaspoon powdered coriander
1 teaspoon salt
Pinch cayenne pepper
2 teaspoons red wine vinegar
Tomatoes and scallions for garnish

Mix the ground lamb with the onions.

Add the cumin, coriander, salt, pepper, and vinegar, and knead the mixture with your hands until it is well blended. Chill it in the refrigerator for 30 minutes.

Wet your hands and form the ground lamb into thin sausage-shaped patties, about 3–4 inches long, and thread them on metal skewers, preferably flat ones. Do not try to form the patty around the skewer; push the point of the skewer through the formed "sausage" and press it tightly around the skewer. The patty should be long and thin to keep it from falling off the skewer.

Grill or broil for 10–15 minutes.

Slide kebabs off the skewers onto serving plates.

Serves 6.

Serve with quartered tomatoes and sliced scallions. Flatbreads also usually accompany this dish.

🦁 LAMB PATTIES WITH EGGS
(Kijma tukhum)

1 large onion, peeled
1 pound ground lamb
Salt and freshly ground black pepper
2 tablespoons vegetable oil
2 large tomatoes, sliced
3 eggs
2 tablespoons chopped fresh parsley
2 tablespoons chopped fresh coriander
1 tablespoon chopped fresh dill

Chop half of the onion finely and mix with the ground lamb. Add salt and pepper to taste.

Shape the lamb into eight oval patties about 3 inches long each.

Heat the vegetable oil and brown the patties on both sides over medium high heat for about 4 minutes on each side. Remove the patties with a slotted spoon to a plate.

Cut the remaining half of the onion into thin rings and fry it in the liquid from the pan for a few minutes until the onion pieces are golden brown.

Remove the onions with a slotted spoon and discard the fat.

Lightly grease an oven-proof casserole just large enough to hold the patties comfortably.

Place the onions on the bottom and layer the tomatoes over them.

Arrange the patties on top of the tomatoes.

Preheat the oven to 450 degrees.

Beat the eggs and add salt to taste; blend in the parsley, coriander and dill.

Pour the eggs over the patties and bake for about 5 minutes until the eggs are firm.

Serves 4.

This dish is good with fried potatoes and a cucumber or spinach salad.

GRAPE LEAVES WITH GROUND LAMB
(Kovatok duilma)

½ cup rice
¼ pound ground lamb
1 medium onion, peeled and finely chopped
Salt and freshly ground black pepper
Pinch cayenne pepper
⅛ teaspoon powdered cumin
1 jar (8 ounces) grape leaves in brine
3 cups beef or lamb broth
Coriander sprigs
Sour cream or yogurt

Simmer the rice for 10 minutes, until it is partially cooked. Drain well.

Add the rice to the lamb, stir in the onions, salt, black and cayenne pepper, and cumin, and mix well.

Rinse the grape leaves well with cold water and separate them. Place them flat on a work surface, shiny side down. If they are very small place two of them together, overlapping lengthwise.

Put 1 teaspoon of the filling near the stem end of each grape leaf and roll up like a jelly roll towards the tip of the leaf, folding the edges underneath the packet.

Put the stuffed grape leaves in a flame-proof casserole or Dutch oven, seam side down and end to end; this will help to keep the filling from leaking out during cooking. They should be arranged in a fairly tight layer. If you have more than one layer, put some coriander sprigs between the layers to prevent them from sticking to each other.

Pour the broth over them.

Bring to a boil over medium high heat. Reduce the heat, cover, and simmer for about 30 minutes, until the meat is cooked through.

Serve in deep plates with a few spoonfuls of broth for each portion, with sour cream or yogurt on the side.

Makes about 2 dozen duilmas.

The stuffed grape leaves can also be drained and served cold as an appetizer.

🌿 MEAT-STUFFED CABBAGE
(Karam duilma)

12–14 large cabbage leaves
1½ pounds ground beef or lamb
½ cup cooked rice
1 small onion, peeled and chopped
1 tablespoon tomato paste
1 tablespoon minced dill
Salt and freshly ground black pepper to taste
Pinch cayenne pepper
1 egg, slightly beaten
3 cups beef or lamb broth, well seasoned
1 bay leaf
Sour cream or yogurt

Rinse the cabbage leaves in cold water and remove tough bottoms.

Boil the cabbage leaves in salted water for 5–6 minutes.

Combine the ground beef or lamb, rice, onion, tomato paste, dill, salt, black and cayenne pepper and egg.

Place about 2–3 tablespoons of the meat filling on each cabbage leaf and roll up carefully, closing the roll with a long wooden toothpick.

Put the cabbage rolls in a flame-proof, lightly greased casserole and pour the broth over them. Add the bay leaf to the pan.

Bring to a boil on medium heat, and then simmer on low heat for 35–45 minutes, until the meat is cooked through. Remove the toothpicks.

Serve in deep plates with a few spoonfuls of broth over each cabbage roll and with sour cream or yogurt on the side.

Serves 6.

STEAMED BEEF STEW
(Azhabsanda)

½ teaspoon butter
3 medium potatoes, peeled and cubed
Salt and pepper
5 plum tomatoes, thickly sliced
3 medium carrots, peeled and cut into strips 1½ inches
    long by about ½ inch wide
1 large onion, cut into thin semicircular rings
2 pounds beef, peeled and cut into 1½-inch cubes
2 Italian sweet peppers, seeded and cut into rings
½ cup chopped fresh dill
½ cup chopped fresh parsley

Use a pot which will fit into a larger, covered pot. Rub the bottom of the smaller pot with the butter, and put in a layer of half of the potatoes.

Sprinkle the potatoes lightly with salt and pepper, and add a layer of half the tomatoes.

Sprinkle this layer with salt and pepper, and add a layer of half the carrots, followed by a layer of half the onions, then one of half the beef and half of the peppers, sprinkling each layer lightly with salt and pepper.

Combine the dill and parsley, and top the layers with half of the herbs.

Repeat the layers on top of the herbs in the same order, starting with the potatoes.

Sprinkle each with salt and pepper, and finish with the remaining dill and parsley.

Fill the larger pot with water so that it comes up to ¾ of the height of the pot with the food.

110

Place the smaller pot in the larger pot and cover tightly.

Bring the pots to a boil over medium heat; reduce the heat and simmer for 1½–2 hours. Be sure that the lid fits tightly; if not, weigh it down to prevent steam from escaping. Check periodically to be sure that the water has not boiled off or spilled over into the smaller pot.

Taste for seasoning before serving and add salt or pepper as needed.

Serves 6.

This dish is good served with Uzbek flatbread, and with rice or noodles to soak up the juices. It can also be made with lamb; be sure that the lamb is not fatty, and cut off any excess fat. Since the only fat is that contained in the meat, this is a relatively low-calorie dish.

🦁 BEEF AND BLACK RADISH STEW
(Khuplama)

The crunchy radish provides a nice contrast to the soft ground meat and vegetables.

2 tablespoons butter
1 medium onion, peeled and cut into semicircular rings
1 pound coarsely ground beef
1 large clove garlic, peeled and minced
1 black radish, peeled and diced
2 large carrots, peeled and diced
1 medium potato, peeled and diced
2 tablespoons tomato paste
1½ cups beef broth
½ teaspoon sweet paprika
Salt
Freshly ground black pepper
Pinch cayenne pepper
2 tablespoons chopped fresh coriander

In a heavy pot or Dutch oven melt the butter and fry the onion until golden. Add the meat and stir to break it up and to brown well on all sides.

When the meat has lost its pink color, add the garlic, radish, carrots, and potato, stirring over medium-low heat until vegetables are soft. Blend in the tomato paste, and stir in the beef broth.

Sprinkle in the paprika, salt, black pepper and cayenne. Cover the pot and simmer over medium heat for 45 minutes, checking occasionally to see that there is enough liquid. Taste for seasoning.

Place the stew in serving bowls and sprinkle each with the coriander.

Serves 4.

This dish can be served over rice or noodles which will absorb the sauce. It should be accompanied by flatbread.

🌹 STUFFED GROUND BEEF BALLS
(Tukhum duilma)

2 pounds ground beef
1 small onion, peeled and very finely chopped
½ cup fine bread crumbs
1 teaspoon salt
¼ teaspoon freshly ground black pepper
6 hard-boiled eggs, peeled
2 eggs, beaten
Vegetable oil for frying

Mix the ground beef with onions, bread crumbs, salt and pepper.

Carefully wrap each of the hard-boiled eggs in the meat mixture, being sure to cover it completely. Set the meatballs aside for 5 minutes.

Heat the oil until it is hot but not smoking. Dip each ball into the beaten eggs and immediately fry in the hot oil until the meat is well browned. Be sure that the balls do not touch each other.

Drain them on paper towels and serve hot.

Serves 6.

Fried potatoes and quartered tomatoes are a traditional accompaniment to this dish.

🦁 GROUND BEEF KEBAB TASHKENT
(Kijma kabob Toshkent)

2 pounds ground beef
1 egg white
1 teaspoon cumin seeds
1 teaspoon salt (or to taste)
½ teaspoon freshly ground black pepper (or to taste)
2 medium onions, peeled and cut in thick rings
Tomatoes and cucumbers for garnish

Mix the ground beef with the egg white, cumin, salt and pepper, kneading the mixture with your hands until it is well blended.

Chill it in the refrigerator for 30 minutes.

Wet your hands and form the meat into balls the size of a large walnut and thread them on metal skewers, alternating the meat with the onion rings.

Do not try to form the ball around the skewer; push the point of the skewer through the ball of meat and press it tightly around the skewer.

Grill or broil for 8–10 minutes, turning the skewers once.

Put the skewers in a 350-degree oven for 5–7 minutes to cook the meat through. If you need to keep the kebabs warm reduce the heat to 300–325 degrees.

Slide kebabs off the skewers onto serving plates.

Serves 6.

Serve with quartered tomatoes and sliced cucumbers. Flatbreads, celery sticks, and sprigs of fresh dill and parsley are traditional accompaniments.

🌾 MEAT AND QUINCE
(Bekhili zharkop)

1½ pounds beef or lamb, cut into 1-inch cubes
1 large quince, peeled, cored, and cut into ½-inch cubes
1 small onion, peeled and cut into semicircular rings
1 can (15 ounces) crushed tomatoes
Salt
Freshly ground black pepper
¼ teaspoon cumin seeds
¼ teaspoon ground cumin
1 cup water
1 tablespoon chopped fresh parsley
1 tablespoon chopped fresh dill

Place the meat, quince, onion, tomatoes, salt, pepper, cumin seeds and ground cumin in a large Dutch oven or heavy flame-proof casserole.

Pour in the water and bring to a boil.

Reduce the heat, cover, and simmer for 50 minutes.

Just before serving sprinkle with the parsley and dill.

Serves 4.

The quince gives this dish a rather tart flavor. The stew can be served over rice or noodles, or with a cabbage salad on the side.

🌿 MEAT WITH RICE AND BEANS
(Lovia shavla)

Vegetables dominate over the meat in this dish.

3 tablespoons vegetable oil
2 large onions, peeled and diced
½ pound beef for stew, cut into very small
    (¼ to ½-inch) cubes
2 carrots, peeled and cut into thin 1-inch long strips
1 can (15 ounces) crushed tomatoes
2 medium potatoes, peeled and diced
1½ cups water
1 cup cooked white beans
1 cup cooked rice
Salt and freshly ground black pepper
Cayenne pepper
1 tablespoon chopped fresh coriander
1 tablespoon chopped fresh parsley

Heat the oil in a large pot or Dutch oven, and sauté the onions until soft.

Add the meat and cook over medium high heat to brown on all sides.

Lower the heat and add the carrots, tomatoes and potatoes, and stir.

Pour in the water, stirring, and cook on medium heat for 10–15 minutes.

Add the beans and rice, and season with salt, black pepper and cayenne to taste. Simmer for 5 minutes.

Sprinkle with the herbs just before serving.

Serves 4–5.

116

❧ GROUND MEAT, MUNG BEAN AND BEET STEW
(Kiimali mashkichiri)

Vegetables play a much more important role than meat in this dish, which has an unusual combination of ingredients and flavors.

2 tablespoons vegetable oil (divided)
1 large onion, peeled and diced (divided)
1 can (15 ounces) beets, drained and diced
5 cups water
1 cup mung beans, washed and picked over
¾ pound ground beef or lamb
Salt and freshly ground black pepper
Cayenne pepper
1 cup rice
2 tablespoons chopped fresh coriander
1 tablespoon chopped fresh parsley
Red wine vinegar (optional)

Heat 1 tablespoon of the oil in a large pot or Dutch oven, and sauté half of the onion until soft.

Add the beets, stir, and pour in the water.

Bring to a boil and add the mung beans. Reduce the heat to medium low, partially cover the pot and cook for 25 minutes.

While the vegetables are cooking, combine the ground meat with the remaining onion, salt, black pepper and cayenne to taste. The meat should be fairly well spiced to contrast with the blander vegetables.

Stir the rice into the vegetables, and continue to cook, partially covered, for another 25 minutes, stirring occasionally and checking to be sure the mixture does not burn. Add more water if needed.

While the vegetables are simmering, heat the remaining tablespoon oil in a frying pan and put in the meat.

Stir with a wooden fork to break up the pieces, and sauté over medium heat until the meat has lost its pink color and is lightly browned. Do not overcook, or the dish will be dry.

Keep the meat warm in a 300-degree oven. If you need to wait for any length of time before serving, sprinkle a few tablespoons of water over the top to keep the mixture moist.

Drain any excess water from the vegetable mixture, and add a pinch of salt if you like. Do not overseason.

Put the vegetables in batches through a food processor. Process for a few seconds, just enough to blend the ingredients and produce a mixture with the consistency of thick oatmeal, but do not allow it to become a smooth purée. Bits of the beet and rice should still be visible.

Place the vegetable mixture in a flat, thick layer on a large serving platter, and arrange the meat on top.

Sprinkle with the coriander and parsley, and serve with a small pitcher of red wine vinegar on the side.

Serves 6.

To make the dish in advance, place the vegetables in a lightly greased oven-proof casserole, and layer the meat on the top. Reheat for 15–20 minutes in a 350-degree oven and sprinkle with the herbs just before serving.

The vinegar with which this dish is customarily served provides a sharp contrast to the meat and vegetables, but this may not be to everyone's taste. You can substitute yogurt or sour cream.

A cucumber salad, crisp flatbread or bread sticks go well with this dish.

🦚 MEATBALLS WITH CHERRIES
(Olchali kijma guisht)

1¼ pounds ground beef or lamb
1 medium onion, peeled and finely chopped
Salt and freshly ground black pepper
1⅓ cups ripe cherries, pitted
4–6 tablespoons vegetable oil

Combine the meat, onion, salt and pepper, and mix well.

Form the meat into small balls the size of a walnut. Make a hollow in the center of each, put in two cherries, and pinch the edges tightly shut.

Heat the oil and fry the meatballs, several at a time, until browned. Add oil if necessary.

Drain on paper towels.

Place the meatballs in a steamer and steam for 10–14 minutes until the meat is thoroughly cooked.

Serves 4.

This dish is good with boiled white rice and string beans with almonds, or with creamed spinach.

LIVER SHASHLYK
(Zhigar kabob)

1½ pounds beef or calf liver
Salt
Freshly ground black pepper
Ground cumin
Pinch cayenne pepper
2 medium onions, peeled and cut in thin rings
White vinegar

Remove the membrane and tough tissue from the liver, and cut into very small (½-inch) cubes.

Sprinkle the liver generously with salt, black pepper and ground cumin, and a pinch of cayenne. Set the cubes aside for 7–8 minutes.

Thread the liver pieces onto either 3 flat metal skewers or 3 small wooden skewers. (If using wooden ones be sure to soak them in water for 10 minutes to keep them from burning).

Grill under a broiler, over hot coals or on an electric grill for 5–7 minutes on each side, turning once, until crisp and brown on the outside but still slightly pink on the inside. Serve immediately, to prevent the liver from toughening.

Serve with the onion rings, and sprinkle with the white vinegar.

Serves 3.

Good with flatbread and sliced tomatoes.

POULTRY

🌱 CHICKEN SHASHLYK
(Tovuk kebab)

1 large onion, peeled and minced
½ teaspoon salt
½ cup red wine vinegar
¼ cup vegetable oil
½ cup water
1 teaspoon powdered cumin
1 teaspoon powdered coriander
1 teaspoon crushed coriander seeds
3 pounds chicken breast meat, cut into 2-inch squares
3 tablespoons melted butter

Combine the first 8 ingredients (except for the chicken and the melted butter), and mix well.

Place the marinade in a large glass bowl and add the cubed chicken. Allow it to marinate for 8–10 hours or overnight.

Thread the chicken onto skewers. Do not crowd the pieces; they should not touch.

Brush the chicken pieces lightly with the melted butter.

Grill over hot coals or in a broiler until cooked through, about 8–12 minutes.

Serves 6.

Serve with tomato salad and pickles.

🦃 APPLE-STUFFED CHICKEN
(Tovuk dim-dim)

1 roasting chicken (4 pounds)
2 large tart apples, peeled, cored and cut in large chunks
3 tablespoons sour cream
8 tablespoons melted butter
Salt and pepper

Dry the chicken and sprinkle it with salt and pepper.

Stuff with the bird with the apples, and sew up the cavity or or close it with toothpicks.

Arrange the chicken in a roasting pan, brush it all over with the sour cream, and pour 4 tablespoons of the melted butter over it.

Preheat the oven to 400 degrees.

Roast the chicken in the center of the oven for 10 minutes, turn it, baste with the butter and juices, and roast it for another 10 minutes.

Reduce the heat to 375 degrees.

Roast the bird for about 45 more minutes, basting with the juices and adding the remaining butter as needed to keep it moist. The bird is done when the juices which flow when the thigh is pierced with a sharp knife are yellow rather than pink.

Cut the bird into quarters and pour some of the pan juices over each portion.

Serves 4.

❦ QUINCE-STUFFED CHICKEN
(Tovuk buglama)

An unusual and tasty combination of fowl and meat.

1 teaspoon salt
¼ teaspoon freshly ground pepper
1 chicken (3 pounds)
¼ pound ground lamb
2 medium quinces, peeled, cored and chopped into
    ½-inch pieces
1½ tablespoons butter, softened
¾ cup water

Combine the salt and pepper and rub the chicken with the mixture.

Lightly salt the lamb and combine with the quinces.

Stuff the chicken with the lamb and quince mixture, and either truss the bird or close the opening with large toothpicks.

Rub the chicken with the softened butter, and put the water in the roasting pan.

Preheat the oven to 350 degrees.

Roast for 1½ hours, basting occasionally with the water and pan juice mixture. Add more water as needed to keep the chicken from burning.

Serves 4.

This dish is good with steamed rice or egg noodles. Roasting makes for a richer taste, but in Uzbekistan, the dish is often steamed. In that case omit the butter and water, place in a large covered steamer, and steam for 1 hour and 40 minutes, or until done.

❧ STUFFED CORNISH HEN
(*Dumali bedana*)

4 Cornish hens
1 tablespoon salt + additional salt for the stuffing
½ teaspoon freshly ground black pepper + additional
    pepper for the stuffing
½ teaspoon ground cumin
1 pound ground lamb
1 small onion, peeled and diced
¼ cup chopped fresh coriander
1 egg
5 tablespoons butter, melted (divided)

Pat the hens dry with paper towels.

Mix 1 tablespoon salt, ½ teaspoon pepper, and the cumin, and rub the hens with the mixture. Rub a little of the spice inside the cavity as well.

Combine the lamb, onion, coriander, egg, and salt and pepper to taste and mix well.

Divide the mixture into 4 parts and stuff each of the hens. Close the opening with toothpicks.

Preheat the oven to 350 degrees.

Place the hens in a greased roasting pan, and pour 2 tablespoons of the butter over them.

Roast for 45–60 minutes, until the birds are golden brown and the juices run yellow when the hen is pricked with a fork. Baste occasionally with the remaining butter and the pan juices, and add water as needed.

Degrease the pan juices and pour over the hens.

Makes 8 servings of ½ Cornish hen each.

124

This dish is often served with a tomato and lettuce salad. Roasted potatoes make a nice accompaniment.

🌿 STEAMED CHICKEN AND HERBS
(Kazan kebab)

1 chicken (4 pounds)
Salt
2 tablespoons vegetable oil
1 medium onion, peeled and sliced into semicircular rings
Pinch cayenne pepper
½ cup chopped fresh basil
½ cup chopped fresh Italian flat-leaf parsley
½ cup chopped fresh coriander
⅔ cup water

Cut the chicken into serving pieces, removing skin and excess fat.

Sprinkle the pieces lightly with salt and set them aside for 5 minutes.

In a heavy casserole heat the oil and place half the chicken pieces in the pot; put the legs on the bottom, reserving the breasts for the top layer.

Sprinkle with a pinch of cayenne pepper, then cover with half the onion, and layer the mixture with half of the basil, parsley, and coriander.

Top with the remaining pieces of chicken breast meat, sprinkle with an additional pinch of cayenne, cover with the remaining onion and sprinkle with the remaining herbs.

Pour in the water down the side of the casserole, so as not to disturb the greens.

Cover the casserole tightly, and cook on low heat for 50–60 minutes, checking occasionally to be sure there is enough liquid and that the chicken does not stick to the bottom of the pan.

Place a piece of chicken on each plate and pour some of the sauce and herbs over it.

Serves 4.

This dish is good served over plain boiled rice or noodles, with a tomato and cucumber salad on the side. The is a relatively low-calorie dish, since no additional fat is used.

❧ BRAISED CHICKEN
(Tovuk zharkop)

2 tablespoons vegetable oil
1 chicken (3 pounds), cut in serving pieces
1 small onion, peeled and cut into semicircular rings
2 tablespoons tomato paste
2 cups crushed tomatoes, fresh or canned
¾ cup water
Salt and pepper
2 teaspoons chopped fresh dill, divided
4 medium potatoes, peeled and quartered

Heat the oil in a Dutch oven or casserole until it is very hot, and add the chicken pieces.

Brown the chicken quickly on both sides over medium high heat and put in the onion. Cook over medium heat for 5 minutes, stirring to keep the mixture from burning.

Add the tomato paste and crushed tomatoes and cook for another 10 minutes.

Pour in the water, sprinkle with salt and pepper to taste and with 1 teaspoon of the chopped dill.

Bring the mixture to a boil and add the potatoes. Reduce the heat, cover, and simmer until the chicken and potatoes are very tender, about 35 minutes.

Taste for seasoning and sprinkle with salt and pepper as needed. Just before serving sprinkle with the remaining teaspoon of dill.

Serves 4–5.

This dish is good served with Uzbek flatbread and a green salad.

❧ CHICKEN WITH PASTA
(*Tovuk shilpildok*)

4 tablespoons corn oil
1 large onion, peeled and finely chopped
1½ pounds chicken breast, cut into ½-inch cubes
⅔ cup chicken broth
Salt and freshly ground black pepper
½ teaspoon powdered cumin
½ teaspoon cumin seeds, crushed
1 cup tomato sauce
1 sheet lasagna pasta, cooked

Heat the oil and sauté the onion and chicken pieces over medium low heat for 5–6 minutes, until chicken has lost its raw color.

Add the chicken broth, salt, pepper, powdered cumin and cumin seeds, and simmer for another 10 minutes. Blend in the tomato sauce.

Cut the cooked lasagna into 2-inch squares and add to the pot. Stir gently, so as not to break the lasagna.

Serve in bowls with several pieces of pasta in each plate along with pieces of chicken.

Serves 6.

Spiced carrot salad or string beans go well with this dish.

✷ CHICKEN AND POTATOES
(Tovuk zharkop)

2 frying chickens (4 pounds each), cut into serving pieces
2 cans (1 pound each) whole tomatoes, crushed, with juice
1 bay leaf
1 teaspoon ground cumin
1 teaspoon ground coriander
Salt and freshly ground black pepper
Pinch cayenne pepper
4 large potatoes, peeled and sliced
Vegetable oil
½ cup chopped fresh parsley

In a large Dutch oven or casserole combine the chickens, tomatoes, bay leaf, cumin, coriander, salt and pepper to taste and the cayenne pepper.

Cover and simmer over moderate heat for 1 hour. Taste for seasoning, and add salt and pepper as needed.

Fry the potatoes in vegetable oil, drain, and sprinkle with salt. Place the potatoes on the serving plates and arrange the chicken and tomato mixture on top. Sprinkle with parsley.

Serves 8.

Serve with flatbread, a cucumber salad, and string beans or carrots.

CHICKEN STEW
(Tovuk kovurma)

1 chicken (4 pounds), cut into serving pieces
Salt
¼ cup vegetable oil
1 medium onion, peeled and sliced in semicircular rings
1 can (15 ounces) whole tomatoes, with juice
2 tablespoons tomato paste
½ cup water
Freshly ground black pepper
1 bay leaf
3 medium potatoes, peeled and coarsely diced
1 tablespoon chopped fresh parsley
2 tablespoons chopped fresh coriander

Sprinkle the chicken pieces with salt and set aside for 15 minutes.

In a flame-proof Dutch oven or casserole heat the oil and sauté the onion on medium-high until soft, 3–4 minutes.

Add the chicken pieces, and sauté on medium heat until chicken is browned on all sides.

Add the tomatoes, tomato paste, water and pepper, and stir well to crush the tomatoes.

Put in the bay leaf, cover the pot, and simmer for 35 minutes on medium low heat. Check occasionally to be sure mixture does not burn, and add a little water if needed.

Add the potatoes, and cook for another 15–20 minutes.

Remove the bay leaf. Taste for seasoning, and sprinkle each serving with some of the chopped parsley and coriander, and with a twist of freshly ground black pepper.

Serves 4.

🌱 GROUND CHICKEN AND EGGS
(Kijma bijran)

1 medium onion, peeled and cut into quarters
1 clove garlic, peeled
2 carrots, peeled and coarsely sliced
2½ pounds ground chicken
Salt and freshly ground black pepper
4 eggs

Place the onion, garlic and carrots in a food processor and process for a few seconds until the mixture is finely minced but not puréed.

Blend well with the chicken, and add salt and pepper to taste.

Preheat the oven to 350 degrees.

Arrange the meat and vegetable mixture in a shallow well-buttered casserole, and bake for 45 minutes, until top of mixture is golden brown.

Beat the eggs well and pour them on top of the chicken.

Cover the casserole and bake for another 10–15 minutes, until the eggs are set.

Serves 6–8

This dish is good with a fresh tomato-cucumber salad.

FISH

🌿 FISH KEBABS
(Balyk kebab)

3 pounds fish steaks such as sturgeon, swordfish, or
    halibut, cut into 1½-inch cubes
3 tablespoons butter, softened
Freshly ground black pepper
Cayenne pepper

Bring a pot of water to a boil and carefully lower the pieces
of fish into the water with a slotted spoon; simmer for 30
seconds. Do not cook any longer or the fish will start to to
flake and will not stick to the skewers.

Remove from heat and cool slightly.

Rub the pieces with the butter, sprinkle generously with the
black and cayenne pepper, and thread onto metal skewers
(preferably flat ones).

Grill until the fish is done, turning once, about 4–5 minutes
on each side. The length of cooking time will depend on the
consistency of the fish you are using. Do not overcook.

Serves 6.

Fish *shashlyk* is usually served with a tomato and onion salad.

❦ STEAMED FISH
(Dimlama balyk)

2 tablespoons butter
2 pounds cod, halibut or flounder fillets
3 medium onions, peeled and cut into thin rings
2 bay leaves
⅓ cup chopped fresh dill
10 crushed black peppercorns
Salt

Allow the fish to steep in lightly salted water for 20 minutes.

In a heavy pot, large enough to hold the fish, melt the butter over low heat.

Remove from heat.

Place a layer of onion rings on the melted butter, cover with a layer of fish filets and 1 bay leaf, and sprinkle with the dill, peppercorns, and salt.

Repeat the layers of onions, fish, bay leaf, dill, pepper and salt until the ingredients have been used up. (Do not use more than 2 bay leaves, even if there are more than 2 layers).

Carefully pour in just enough water to cover the fish.

Slowly bring the fish to a boil, reduce the heat to very low, cover the pot tightly and simmer until the fish is thoroughly cooked through, 15–25 minutes, depending on the type of fish and its thickness. Test with a fork to see when the fish flakes and is done.

Pour the sauce into a serving dish and serve it with the fish.

Serves 4.

This fish goes well with boiled potatoes and a green salad.

🌿 FRIED FISH (SMELTS)
(Kovurma balyk)

1½ pounds smelts
Vegetable oil
4 cloves garlic, peeled and crushed
½ teaspoon salt
1 tablespoon chopped fresh parsley
1 tablespoon chopped fresh dill
Flour for dredging
2 eggs

Remove the heads and the single bone from the smelts.

Combine ⅓ cup oil, the garlic, salt, parsley and dill in a flat glass dish.

Put in the smelts and toss to moisten all the fish in the marinade.

Refrigerate for 1–2 hours, and drain the fish well.

Dredge the fish in flour, shaking off the excess.

Beat the eggs well, and dip the fish into the eggs, allowing excess to drip off.

Heat ½ cup oil until it is very hot and fry the fish a few pieces at a time (do not crowd them), until crisp and golden brown.

Drain on paper towels and keep hot in a lightly buttered casserole in a 325-degree oven until ready to serve.

Serves 4.

🌿 FRIED FISH WITH HERBS
(Kovurma balyk va kuikat)

2 pounds fish fillets (flounder, cod, halibut), cut into
  2-inch squares
2 large cloves garlic, peeled and crushed
¼ cup chopped fresh parsley
¼ cup chopped fresh dill
Salt and freshly ground black pepper
6 tablespoons vegetable oil (approximately)
2 medium onions, peeled and cut into rings

Place the fish in a colander and run cold water over it.

Combine the garlic, parsley, dill, salt and pepper, and mix well.

Rub the pieces of fish with the mixture and set them aside in the refrigerator for 1 hour.

Heat 2 tablespoons of the oil and fry the onion rings until they are golden brown. Remove them with a slotted spoon and keep hot in a low oven.

In a separate pan heat the remaining oil until it is very hot and fry the pieces of fish for a few minutes until cooked through.

Drain on paper towels, and serve with the onion rings.

Serves 4.

Serve with fresh tomato wedges and cucumber slices.

🦂 FRIED FISH WITH GARLIC
(Kovurma balyk va sarymsok)

18 smelts or 12 small whiting or 2 large carp, cut into
    1-inch pieces
Flour for dredging
½ cup vegetable oil
⅔ cup water
1 teaspoon salt
4 cloves garlic, peeled and crushed
⅔ cup chopped coriander

Dry the fish thoroughly and dredge lightly with flour, shaking off the excess.

Heat the oil until it is very hot and fry the fish over moderate heat for about 5 minutes, turning the pieces.

Remove fish from pan and place on paper towels to absorb excess oil, and remove the fish to a shallow dish.

In a small pot combine the water, salt, and garlic, and heat until just warm; add ½ cup of the coriander, and pour the sauce over the fish.

Let the pieces soak for 5 minutes on one side, then turn and allow them to soak on the other side.

Serve at once garnished with remaining coriander. The dish should be served at room temperature.

Serves 6.

❧ FISH CUTLETS PO-MUNAISKI
(*Muinokcha balyk kotleti*)

1 pound white-fleshed fish (such as flounder, turbot or cod)
1 small onion, peeled and quartered
2 tablespoons sour cream
1 egg, slightly beaten
½ teaspoon salt or to taste
Freshly ground black pepper
2 tablespoons flour + flour for dredging
⅓ cup vegetable oil (approximately)
½ cup water or fish broth
¼ cup chopped parsley
2 scallions (green parts only), chopped

Cut the fish coarsely and put it through a food processor along with the onion, pulsing until the mixture forms a rough mass but not a purée. Be careful not to overprocess; you should see small pieces of onion in the mixture.

Blend in the sour cream and the egg, stirring with a wooden spoon, and add salt and pepper to taste.

Stir in the 2 tablespoons flour.

Wet your hands and form the mixture into oval patties about 2 inches in diameter.

Dredge them lightly with flour, shaking off the excess, and set the patties aside for 5 minutes.

Heat the oil until it is very hot, and sauté the patties on fairly high heat for about 5 minutes on each side, until they are crisp and golden.

Reduce the heat, pour off the fat from the skillet, add the water or broth, and simmer for 3 to 4 minutes.

Combine the chopped parsley and scallions.

With a slotted spoon remove the fish to a serving platter and sprinkle with the chopped greens.

Makes 12 cutlets.

The fish cutlets can be served with mashed or boiled potatoes, or steamed pumpkin or squash.

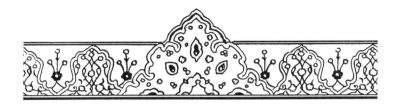

PLOVS

P*lovs* or *palovs*, as they are called in Uzbek, are the crowning glory of Uzbek national cuisine. A relative of the pilafs of Armenia, Iran, Azerbaijan and the Middle East, *palov* is the best known and best loved national dish. Though Uzbek men generally leave the cooking to women, until the Revolution of 1917 *plov* was a man's affair. In the 1960s a member of the Central Committee of the Soviet Communist Party for whom I was interpreting shocked his American hosts by stating that as far as he was concerned one of the most significant achievements of the 1917 Revolution was that it finally gave Uzbek women the right to make *plov*.

There are more than 400 recipes for *plov* in Uzbek cooking, and every housewife seems to have her own special recipe. There is *plov* with quince, pumpkin, egg, meatballs, garlic, chickpeas, turnips, raisins and dried apricots, to name only a few of the dishes.

The lamb fat from a fat-tailed sheep (*kurdiuk*)—and plenty of it—is used in making a traditional *plov*. A very tasty dish, however, can be prepared using a minimum of fat, and vegetable oils such as corn oil make a quite acceptable substitute. Do not use olive oil, however, as the taste will dominate the subtle blend of flavors of the *plov*. At the outset the fat—(and this can be only a few tablespoons of vegetable oil)—is melted or rendered in a heavy pot. Onions and carrots are sautéed in it, and then the meat is added. Spices are sprinkled in after the mixture, known as the *zirvak*, has been simmered on low heat to blend the flavors of all the ingredients. Then the rice and water are carefully added, so as not to disturb the layer of ingredients on the bottom, for a *plov* is never stirred. The pot is covered tightly, and the mixture cooked until the water has boiled away. Use an asbestos pad or flame tamer to keep the mixture from burning, and add water if needed.

Plovs take patience, and this process cannot be rushed; otherwise, you will wind up with soggy or burned rice. If the *plov* is made in advance it can be held in the oven at 275 degrees, and a little water can be added if it starts to dry out. The rice is then ladled out onto each plate, with some of the *zirvak* spooned on top.

Uzbekistan has hundreds of varieties of rice, and many different kinds are used in making *plovs*. Basmati rice, or any short or medium grained rice such as one of the Japanese varieties work well for these recipes.

A *plov* is a meal in itself, but it is usually served with an assortment of vegetable salads, a plate of herbs such as parsley and coriander sprigs, fresh radishes and cucumbers. For American dinners, a Cabernet goes nicely with a lamb *plov*, and a light white Bordeaux or Chardonnay can accompany a chicken *plov*. Fresh fruit or a fruit compote with cookies is a good dessert following this filling dish. Green tea can be served with the plov as well as with dessert.

LAMB PLOV
(Kovurma palov)

(Adapted from Anya von Bremzen and John Welchman, *Please to the Table*: New York, Workman Publishing, 1990)

½ cup vegetable oil (such as corn oil)
1 pound lamb meat, cut into 1½-inch cubes
5 carrots, peeled and cut into thick strips
3 large onions, peeled and coarsely chopped
1 teaspoon paprika
¼ teaspoon ground turmeric
2 teaspoons cumin seeds
Salt and freshly ground black pepper to taste
½ cup water
2 cups short, medium grain or basmati rice
1 whole medium-sized head of garlic, peeled, with
        outer stem removed
4 cups boiling water

Heat the oil in a large, heavy casserole or Dutch oven.

Add the lamb and brown it well on all sides, stirring frequently, for 6–8 minutes.

Add the carrots and the onion and cook until the onions turn golden.

Stir in the paprika, turmeric, cumin seeds, salt, and pepper. Add the ½ cup water.

Bring the mixture to a boil, reduce the heat to medium low, and simmer until the meat is tender, about 2 minutes. Check to be sure the mixture does not burn.

Flatten the surface of the meat mixture with a large spoon.

Pour the rice over the meat and bury the head of garlic in it.

Flatten the top of the rice.

Carefully pour in the boiling water down the side of the mixture, so that that the rice does not blend with the meat mixture.

Let the water pot boil at fairly high heat until the water has evaporated, about 15–20 minutes.

Poke several holes in the rice with the handle of a wooden spoon. This will allow the water on the bottom of the pan to evaporate.

Reduce the heat to very low, cover the pot tightly and steam the *plov* until the rice is tender, about 20–30 minutes. You may use a flame tamer or asbestos pad to keep the *plov* from burning.

Remove from the heat and let it stand for 5 minutes before serving.

Put the rice on a large serving platter and mound the meat, vegetables and garlic over it.

Serves 6.

QUINCE PLOV
(Bekhili palov)

Add 1 large quince, cored, peeled and diced to the *zirvak* while it is cooking. If you cannot obtain quince, try 2 large tart apples, peeled, cored and diced.

CHICKPEA PLOV
(Nujkhotli palov)

Add 1½ cups canned and well-drained chickpeas to the *zirvak* while it is cooking.

🌿 GARLIC PLOV
(Sarimsok palov)

Add 15 peeled cloves of garlic to the *zirvak* while it is cooking. Omit the garlic buried in the rice.

🌿 PUMPKIN PLOV
(Oshkovok palov)

Add 1½ cups diced fresh pumpkin to the *zirvak* while it is cooking.

🌿 SQUASH PLOV
(Oshkovok palov)

Add 1½ cups diced yellow zucchini to the *zirvak* while it is cooking.

🌿 TURNIP PLOV
(Shalgamli palov)

Add 1½ cups turnips, peeled and cut into 1½-inch strips ¼ inch wide, to the *zirvak* while it is cooking.

🌿 TURNIP AND WHITE RADISH PLOV
(Shalgamli va rediska palov)

Replace the carrots in the basic Lamb *Plov* with 1½ cups peeled turnips, cut into strips 1½ inches long and ¼ inch wide and with 1½ cups white radish, peeled and cut into strips of similar size. Soak the white radish strips for 20 minutes in cold salted water and drain well before cooking. Pat dry with paper towels. Do not fry the mixture with the radish strips for too long, as they may burn or toughen.

🌿 DRIED APRICOT PLOV
(Urikli palov)

Add 1 cup coarsely chopped dried apricots, soaked for 45 minutes in warm water and well drained, to the *plov* right before adding the rice.

🌿 RAISIN PLOV
(Majizli palov)

Add 1 cup black raisins, soaked in warm water for 45 minutes and well drained, to the *zirvak* while it is cooking.

🌿 PASTA PLOV
(Ugra palov)

Replace the rice with an equal amount of orzo and a tablespoon of butter. Check on the water while the dish is steaming; you may need to add a bit more water.

NOTES ON PLOVS

You can also use various combinations of these ingredients, e.g. quince and chickpea, or pumpkin and raisin, etc.

If you like a spicier dish, a pinch of cayenne pepper can be added to the *zirvak*. You can also add an extra teaspoon of ground coriander or crushed coriander seeds, or a pinch of saffron.

❧ "ABUNDANCE" PLOV
(Bairam palovi)

½ cup vegetable oil
3 pounds lamb, cut into 1½-inch cubes
3 medium onions, peeled and diced
4 large carrots, peeled and cut into 1½-inch strips
1 quince, peeled and diced, or 1 large apple, peeled, cored and coarsely chopped
½ cup canned chickpeas, drained
½ cup golden raisins
⅓ cup dried apricots, coarsely chopped
2½ teaspoons crushed cumin seeds
1 teaspoon paprika
4 cloves garlic, peeled and coarsely sliced
Salt and pepper
2½ cups rice, washed and drained (medium-grain or basmati)
3–4 cups boiling water + additional water
2 tablespoons chopped fresh coriander
1 tablespoon chopped fresh parsley

Heat the oil until it is very hot.

Add the lamb meat and brown well on all sides over medium high heat, stirring constantly. Put in the onions and carrots and continue to cook on high heat for another 7–8 minutes, until the onions are soft and golden.

Reduce the heat, and add the quince or apple, chickpeas, raisins, apricots, cumin, paprika, garlic, and salt and pepper to taste.

Pour in ⅔ cup water, bring the mixture to a boil, lower the heat, cover the pot and simmer for about 30 minutes.

Taste for seasoning and adjust as needed.

Flatten the top of the mixture with a spatula, and sprinkle the rice evenly over the meat and vegetables.

Carefully pour in the boiling water down the side of the pot, to keep the rice from mixing with the meat. Do not stir.

Raise the heat, and let the water boil off, for about 10 minutes. Watch the *plov* carefully to keep it from burning, and add more water if necessary,

When the water has boiled off make several holes through the rice with the handle of a wooden spoon. Reduce the heat to low, cover the casserole, and simmer for another 20 minutes, until the rice is tender. Use a flame tamer or asbestos pad to keep the *plov* from burning. Check to see that the meat does not burn, and add water if needed.

Spread the rice on a large platter, and mound the meat and vegetables on top of the rice.

Sprinkle the *plov* with the chopped coriander and parsley.

Serves 8–10.

Serve with a fresh vegetable salad and an Uzbek flatbread.

🌿 BUKHARAN BEEF PLOV
(*Guishti palov*)

¾ cup vegetable oil
3 large onions, peeled and finely chopped
1½ pounds beef for stew, cut into 1-inch cubes
6 carrots, peeled and cut into thick strips
2½ cups rice
3 cups boiling water (approximately)
Salt and pepper to taste
2 teaspoons ground turmeric
2 teaspoons cumin seeds
½ teaspoon ground cumin

Heat the oil in a large, heavy casserole or Dutch oven.

Sauté the onions for 4–5 minutes over low heat, and then add the beef.

Brown it well on all sides, stirring frequently, for 10–12 minutes.

Layer the carrots on top of the meat and onion mixture, but do not stir.

Put the rice on top of the carrots, and carefully pour in the boiling water down the side of the pot. It should come to 1 inch over the surface of the rice.

Sprinkle with the salt, pepper, turmeric, cumin seeds and cumin, and stir carefully so that the spices blend only with the rice, and the meat and vegetables remain undisturbed.

Bring the mixture to a boil, reduce the heat to medium low, cover the pot and simmer for 40 minutes, until most of the water has evaporated. Check to be sure the mixture does not burn.

Let the water pot boil at fairly high heat until the water has evaporated, about 15–20 minutes.

Poke several holes in the rice with the handle of a wooden spoon to allow the water on the bottom of the pan to evaporate.

Fluff up the rice layer without touching the vegetables or meat. Reduce the heat to very low, cover the pot tightly and steam the *plov* until the rice is tender, about 20–30 minutes more.

Remove from the heat and let it stand for 5 minutes before serving.

Put the rice on a large serving platter and mound the meat and vegetables over it.

Serves 6.

MEATBALL PLOV
(Kijma palov)

½ cup vegetable oil
5 carrots, peeled and cut into thick strips
3 large onions, peeled and coarsely chopped
1 teaspoon paprika
¼ teaspoon ground turmeric
2 teaspoons cumin seeds
Salt and freshly ground pepper to taste
¼ cup water
1 recipe Ground Beef Kebabs Tashkent (p. 114), uncooked
2 cups rice
8 cloves garlic, peeled
3 cups boiling water

Heat the oil in a large, heavy casserole or Dutch oven.

Add the carrots and the onion and cook until the onions turn golden.

Stir in the paprika, turmeric, cumin seeds, salt, and pepper. Add the ¼ cup water.

Bring the mixture to a boil, reduce the heat to medium low, and simmer for 8–10 minutes. Check to be sure the mixture does not burn.

Flatten the surface of mixture with a large spoon. Put the meatballs on top of the vegetables.

Pour the rice over the meatballs and push the garlic cloves into it.

Flatten the top of the rice.

Carefully pour in the boiling water down the side of the mixture, so that that the rice does not blend with the meat mixture.

Let the water pot boil at fairly high heat until the water has evaporated, about 15–20 minutes.

Poke several holes in the rice with the handle of a wooden spoon. This will allow the water on the bottom of the pan to evaporate.

Reduce the heat to very low, cover the pot tightly and steam the *plov* until the rice is tender, about 20–30 minutes.

Remove from the heat and let it stand for 5 minutes before serving.

Put the rice on a large serving platter and mound the meatballs, vegetables and garlic over it.

Serves 6.

🌺 STUFFED GRAPE LEAVES PLOV
(Kovatuk palov)

½ cup vegetable oil
5 carrots, peeled and cut into thick strips
3 large onions, peeled and coarsely chopped
¼ teaspoon ground turmeric
2 teaspoons cumin seeds
½ teaspoon ground cumin
Salt and freshly ground black pepper to taste
½ cup water
1½ cups rice
8 cloves garlic, peeled
2½ cups boiling water
1 recipe for stuffed Grape Leaves with Ground Lamb
    (see p. 107)

Heat the oil in a large, heavy casserole or Dutch oven.

Sauté the carrots and the onion and cook until the onions turn golden.

Stir in the turmeric, cumin seeds, ground cumin, salt, and pepper. Add the ½ cup water.

Bring the mixture to a boil, reduce the heat to medium low, and simmer for 5–8 minutes. Check to be sure the mixture does not burn.

Flatten the surface of the vegetable mixture with a large spoon.

Pour the rice over the vegetables and bury the garlic in it.

Flatten the top of the rice.

Carefully pour in the boiling water down the side of the mixture, so that that the rice does not blend with the vegetables.

Let the food in the pot boil at fairly high heat until the water has evaporated, about 15–20 minutes.

Poke several holes in the rice with the handle of a wooden spoon. This will allow the water on the bottom of the pan to evaporate.

Reduce the heat to very low, cover the pot tightly and steam the *plov* until the rice is tender, about 20–30 minutes.

Remove from the heat and let it stand for 5 minutes before serving.

Put the rice on a large serving platter and mound the vegetables and garlic over it. Arrange the cooked stuffed grape leaves decoratively on top of the vegetables.

Serves 6.

Variation: Stuff the grape leaves but do not cook them. Place them on top of the vegetables before putting in the rice, and let them cook together with the rice and vegetables. Put the rice on a serving platter and cover with the vegetables and stuffed grape leaves

STUFFED CABBAGE PLOV
(Karam duilma palov)

Proceed as above, but substitute 1 recipe for Meat-Stuffed Cabbage (see p. 109) for the stuffed grape leaves.

❧ CHICKEN PLOV
(Tovuk palov)

2 frying chickens, cut into serving pieces
6 tablespoons vegetable oil
3 medium onions, peeled and thinly sliced
6 carrots, peeled and cut into thick strips
5 cups water, divided
Salt and freshly ground black pepper
2 cups rice

Dry the chicken pieces.

In a heavy casserole or Dutch oven heat the oil and brown the chicken pieces on all sides.

Add the onion slices and sauté until golden.

Add the carrots and cook for 5 minutes.

Add 3 cups water, salt and pepper to taste, raise the heat slightly, and bring the mixture to a boil.

Lower the heat, cover and simmer until the chicken is tender, adding water if necessary to keep the food from burning.

Place the rice on top of the chicken, and carefully pour in the remaining water so as not to disturb it.

Bring to a boil, reduce the heat, and simmer on fairly high heat until the water has evaporated, about 15–20 minutes.

Push the rice towards the center of the pot and poke holes in several places with the handle of a wooden spoon.

Cover and cook over low heat until the rice is done and all of the water has evaporated (about 25 minutes). Use a flame tamer or asbestos pad to keep the *plov* from burning. Place the rice on a serving platter and mound the chicken and *zirvak* on top.

Serves 8.

❧ BUKHARAN CHICKEN PLOV
(Tovuk palov)

(Adapted from Anya von Bremzen and John Welchman, *Please to the Table*, New York: Workman Publishing, 1990).

2 frying chickens, cut into 12 pieces
⅓ cup vegetable oil (approximately)
2 medium onions, chopped
3 large carrots, peeled and diced
1 large tart apple, peeled, cored and diced
1 large quince, peeled, cored and diced (If you cannot
    find quinces use 2 apples)
1¼ cups raisins
1 teaspoon crushed cumin seeds
¼ teaspoon ground cinnamon
4 cups chicken stock
Salt and freshly ground black pepper
2 cups rice

Dry the chicken pieces well.

Heat about half of the oil in a heavy Dutch oven or skillet and brown the chicken pieces (a few at a time) on all sides.

Remove pieces from the pan as soon they are browned, add the remaining pieces, and more oil, if needed.

In another large, heavy casserole heat 2 tablespoons oil, add the onions and carrots, and sauté until the onions are golden, about 10 minutes.

Add the apple and quince and continue to cook for 10 more minutes on low heat.

Put in the browned chicken pieces, raisins, cumin, cinnamon, ½ cup of stock and salt and pepper to taste. Cover the pot and simmer for 20 minutes.

Place the rice on top of the mixture, pour the remaining stock carefully down the side so as not to disturb the mixture, and boil, uncovered, for about 10 minutes over fairly high heat until the stock is absorbed.

Mound the rice in the center of the pot and poke several holes in it with the handle of a wooden spoon. Cover tightly, reduce the heat to very low, and steam the rice until it is tender, about 30 minutes. You may put an asbestos pad under the pot to keep the mixture from burning as the stock evaporates.

Allow the *plov* to stand for 5 minutes. Arrange the rice on a serving plate and mound the chicken and vegetables on top.

Serves 6.

❧ HERB PLOV
(Kuikat palov)

(Courtesy of Uzbekistan Tandoori Bread Bakery)

2 tablespoons vegetable oil
1 medium onion, peeled and finely chopped
½ pound ground lamb or beef
Salt and freshly ground black pepper
Pinch saffron
1 cup chopped fresh parsley
1 cup chopped fresh coriander
½ chopped fresh mint
½ cup chopped fresh dill
1½ cups rice

Heat the oil and sauté the onion until golden.

Add the meat, stirring to break it up. Sprinkle in the salt, pepper and saffron.

156

Cook for 12–15 minutes on medium low heat, stirring to keep from burning.

Pour in 2 cups of water. Bring the pot to a boil.

Add ¾ cup of the parsley, ¼ cup coriander, and half of the mint and dill to the meat and onion. Stir briefly and simmer on low heat, covered, for 15 minutes.

Place the rice in a colander and pour cold water over it.

Add the rice to the pot and press the ingredients down with the back of a spoon.

Add more water so that the mixture is covered by at least 1 inch of water.

Cover the pot tightly and bring the mixture to a boil.

Lower the heat and cook until all the water has evaporated, about 20 minutes.

Sprinkle with the remaining herbs just before serving.

Serves 6.

Note: This *plov* can be made without the meat and served as an accompaniment to a meat or chicken dish.

🥬 TOMATO AND EGG PLOV
(Pomidor kuimokli palov)

½ cup vegetable oil
5 carrots, peeled and cut into thick strips
3 large onions, peeled and coarsely chopped
¼ teaspoon ground turmeric
2 teaspoons crushed cumin seeds
Salt and freshly ground black pepper to taste
1 cup water
6 very ripe tomatoes
2½ cups boiling water
6 eggs

Heat the oil in a large, heavy casserole (cast iron or a Dutch oven is fine).

Add the carrots and the onion and cook until the onions turn golden.

Stir in the turmeric, cumin seeds, salt, and pepper.

Add 1 cup water. Bring the mixture to a boil, reduce the heat to medium low, and simmer for 15 minutes.

Cut off the stem end of the tomato, and scoop out the tomato pulp, leaving a thick shell.

Sprinkle the insides of the tomato shells with salt.

Flatten the surface mixture in the pan with a large spoon. Pour the rice over it and flatten the top.

Carefully pour in the 2½ cups boiling water down the side of the mixture, taking care that the rice does not blend with the vegetable mixture.

Turn up the heat and let the water boil at fairly high heat until it has all evaporated, about 15–20 minutes.

Poke several holes in the rice with the handle of a wooden spoon. This will allow the water on the bottom of the pan to evaporate.

Reduce the heat to low.

Crack one egg into each of the tomato shells, sprinkle them with salt and pepper, and carefully place the tomatoes in the pot on top of the rice.

Cover the pot tightly and steam the *plov* until the rice is tender, about 20–25 minutes. Remove from the heat and let it stand for 5 minutes.

Carefully remove the tomatoes.

Put the rice on a large serving platter and arrange the vegetables on top. Surround the dish with the tomatoes.

Serves 6.

STUFFED PASTRIES, DUMPLINGS, PASTA AND PANCAKES

Small parcels of dough stuffed with meat and various other fillings are a component of almost every cuisine on the globe, and Uzbek cooking is no exception; various kinds of stuffed pastries and dumplings are some of the most popular dishes in Uzbekistan. The large steamed dumplings, *manty*, are filled with meat or vegetables, and steamed in a *mantychnitsa*, a tiered steamer which holds the dumplings on several perforated sheets of metal over boiling water. The smaller *chuchvara* dumplings, relatives of Russian *pelmeni*, are usually boiled. The dumplings are often served with vinegar, sour cream or yogurt sauce.

Round or triangular pies ranging from 2 to 6 inches in diameter, called *samsas* (the word is related to the *samosas* of India), are relatives of Russian *pirozhki*. These are baked or fried, and filled with lamb, greens, and rice and vegetable mixtures. The meat for *samsas* and *manty* should be chopped into tiny ¼-inch cubes. The meat should be kept for 30 minutes in the freezer right before cutting, to make it easier to chop. Cut into thin slices and then cut crosswise to cube. Or the meat can be processed into pieces the size of peas by pulsing for a few seconds in a food processor, taking care to avoid grinding it into a homogeneous mass. For *chuchvara*, however, the meat should be ground until it has the consistency of hamburger meat. Purchased ground meat can be used for this purpose. The filling will be more moist if you press down hard with both hands on the chopped onions in a bowl to extract their juice. The cumin seeds will release their fragrance when placed in a small plastic bag and crushed with a few strokes of a rolling pin or a can rolled on its side. Don't hesitate to combine the various doughs and fillings and to experiment with new fillings.

The influence of Chinese cuisine is strongly felt in the noodles and pasta dishes which are extremely popular in Uzbek cooking. While home-made pasta can be used in any and all of these dishes, most American cooks prefer to use ready-made store-bought pasta, which works perfectly well in these recipes. Noodles are boiled in water or meat broth, or sometimes fried, and are served with meat sauce, in thick stews and in soups. Pasta is cut into squares or formed into small balls, and is a common ingredient in meat and vegetable dishes. *Lagman*, the meat, noodle and carrot soup, can be made with less broth and served as a stew.

❧ STEAMED LAMB DUMPLINGS 1
(Manty)

(Recipe adapted from Anya von Bremzen and John Welchman, *Please to The Table*, New York: Workman Publishing, 1990)

DOUGH
2 cups unbleached flour
½ teaspoon salt
2 large egg yolks, beaten
1 tablespoon vegetable oil
7–8 tablespoons water

FILLING

1½ pounds lamb from shoulder or leg, finely chopped
    into pea-size pieces
2 medium onions, peeled and chopped
⅓ cup lamb stock or beef broth
½ cup chopped fresh coriander
Salt to taste
1½ teaspoons freshly ground black pepper
8 tablespoons (1 stick) unsalted butter, cut into
    small pieces

Mix the flour and salt for the dough. (You can do this in a food processor).

Beat in the egg yolks and oil and add the water, mixing or pulsing in the processor until a dough ball forms.

Place the dough on a floured board and knead until it is smooth, about 2 or 3 minutes.

Cover with a kitchen towel and set the dough aside for 30 minutes.

In a large bowl mix together the ground lamb, onions, lamb or beef stock, coriander, salt and pepper.

Divide the dough into 2 balls.

Roll out 1 ball of dough on a floured ball to a thickness of about ¹⁄₁₆-inch; the dough will be very thin.

Cut out 4-inch circles of dough, and heap about 2 tablespoons of filling in the center of the circle. Do not put in too much filling to prevent the dumplings from opening while steaming.

Fold up the sides around each circle. (If you are using the optional butter, put a small piece on top of the filling now. This gives the dumplings a much richer taste and makes them more moist, though of course this adds calories).

Wet your fingers with cold water and pinch the edges of the *manty* together tightly on top.

Roll out the other ball of dough and repeat the same process.

Grease the bottom tier of a steamer, and bring 2 inches of water to a boil. Place the *manty* in the steamer, being sure they do not touch. Cover tightly and steam for 20 minutes.

Serves 6 (24 manty*).*

These can be served with Yogurt Sauce (p. 195), with black pepper freshly ground onto the *manty*, white vinegar or Spiced White Vinegar (p. 195).

STEAMED LAMB DUMPLINGS 2
(Manty)

(Courtesy of Boris Eliyukin and Elena Granovskiy)

DOUGH
4½–5 cups flour
1 teaspoon salt
1 egg, lightly beaten
1½ cups cold water

FILLING
1½ pounds fatty lamb from shoulder or leg
2 medium onions, peeled
1 teaspoon salt
½ teaspoon freshly ground black pepper
1 teaspoon cumin seeds
¼ cup flour
¼ cup water

Combine 4 cups flour with 1 teaspoon salt.

Place the egg and 1½ cups water in a large bowl and beat slightly.

Gradually add the flour, stirring, until the dough forms a ball which can be kneaded and does not stick to your hands.

Mix by hand or in a processor until the dough forms a ball.

Place the dough in a bowl, cover with a small bowl placed upside down, and allow it to rest for 30 minutes.

Put the lamb in the freezer for ½ hour before using. Cut into thin strips and cut the strips crosswise into ¼-inch cubes

Cut the onions into thin strips and then cut the strips crosswise into ¼ inch pieces.

Place the onions in a large bowl and press down hard with your hands, squeezing to extract the juice. This will make the filling more moist.

Add the lamb to the onions, and stir in the salt and pepper.

Place the cumin seeds on a piece of wax paper, cover with more paper, and crush them briefly with a rolling pin; this will release their fragrance. Add them to the lamb.

Work the ¼ cup flour into the meat and then blend in the ¼ cup water.

Roll out the dough on a lightly floured board to 1/16-inch thickness and cut into 4-inch circles.

Place about 2 tablespoons of filling in the center of each circle.

Pinch the ends of the dough together tightly on top of each dumpling.

Grease a steamer and steam the dumplings over 2 inches of hot water for 30–40 minutes.

Serves 6.
Makes 15–20 manty.

Serve with Yogurt Sauce (p. 195), sour cream, white vinegar or Spiced White Vinegar (p. 195). The *manty* can also be sprinkled with freshly ground black pepper and with chopped fresh parsley, dill and coriander.

🦂 BROWNED LAMB DUMPLINGS IN BROTH
(*Manty*)

1 recipe for dough and filling for Steamed Lamb
    Dumplings (*Manty*) 2 (p. 167)
8–12 tablespoons butter (approximately)
6 cups lamb or beef broth
2 tablespoons chopped fresh parsley
2 tablespoons chopped fresh dill
2 tablespoons chopped fresh coriander

Make the *manty*, using dough and filling as in Steamed Lamb Dumplings (*Manty*) 2.

Heat 8 tablespoons butter over medium heat in a large saucepan until it just starts to brown.

Fry the *manty* gently for a few minutes, until they are brown on all sides, adding butter as needed.

Remove the *manty* with a slotted spoon, and steam as in the recipe for Steamed Dumplings (*Manty*) 2. (This is important, because the meat filling will still be raw after the frying process).

Heat the beef broth and divide between 6 deep bowls.

Place a few dumplings in each bowl.

Combine the parsley, dill and coriander, and sprinkle over each portion.

Serves 6.

🦢 STEAMED BEEF DUMPLINGS
(Manty)

DOUGH
3 cups unbleached flour
Pinch salt
1½ cups water

FILLING
1½ pounds beef (stew beef or round), finely chopped into
    ¼-inch cubes or pea-size pieces
2 medium onions, finely chopped
Salt
1 teaspoon freshly ground black pepper
1 tablespoon chopped fresh dill
4 tablespoons butter, cut into very small pieces (optional)

In a large bowl combine the flour and salt. Make a well in the center and add the water.

Mix well, and then work the dough either by hand or in a processor until it forms a ball.

Leave the dough in a covered bowl to rest for 10 minutes.

Combine the beef, onions, salt, pepper and dill and mix well.
170

Roll out the dough on a floured board to ¹⁄₁₆-inch thickness.

Cut into 4-inch circles and place 2 tablespoons of filling in the center of each.

If you are using the butter, put a small piece on the top of each of the manty. (This will yield a richer taste and a moister dumpling, though it obviously adds calories).

Wet your fingers with cold water and pinch the edges of the dumpling tightly shut on top.

Steam the *manty* in a lightly greased steamer with 2 inches of water on the bottom for about 20 minutes.

Makes about 20–22 manty.

Can be served with Yogurt Sauce (see p. 195), sprinkled with more fresh dill, or with white vinegar or Spiced White Vinegar (p. 195).

❧ CHICKEN DUMPLINGS
(Tovuk gushtli manty)

DOUGH
1 *manty* dough recipe for Steamed Lamb Dumplings
(*Manty*) 1 (p. 165)

FILLING
1½ pounds chicken meat, chopped into ¼-inch cubes or
    processed into pea-size pieces in food processor
2 medium onions, peeled and chopped
⅓ cup chicken broth
½ cup chopped fresh coriander
Salt to taste
½ teaspoon fresh ground black pepper

Mix all the ingredients for the filling, and proceed as in Steamed Lamb Dumplings (*Manty*) 1.

Serves 6 (24 manty*).*

The *manty* can be served with sour cream or yogurt on the side.

🦎 SQUASH DUMPLINGS
(Oshkovok manty)

DOUGH
1 recipe for dough from Steamed Lamb Dumplings
    (*Manty*) 1 (p. 165)

FILLING
1 recipe for Squash *Samsa (Oshkovok samsa)* filling (p. 186)

Make the dough and filling, and proceed as in Steamed Lamb Dumplings (*Manty*) 1

Serves 6 (24 manty*).*

Serve with Yogurt Sauce (p. 195) or sour cream on the side.

🌿 TURNIP MANTY
(Turpli manty)

1 recipe for dough from Steamed Lamb Dumplings
    (*Manty*) 1 (p. 165)
2 large turnips, peeled
1 pound beef or lamb, cut into ¼-inch cubes or finely
    chopped into pea-size pieces
2 medium onions, peeled and chopped
⅓ cup lamb or beef broth
Salt to taste
1½ teaspoons freshly ground black pepper
⅛ teaspoon cayenne pepper
8 tablespoons (1 stick) unsalted butter, cut into small pieces
    (optional)

Cut the turnips into eighths and soak the pieces in salt water
for 45 minutes.

Drain well and chop into pea-sized pieces.

Combine the turnips with the meat, onions, meat broth, salt
and black and cayenne pepper.

Fill the *manty* as in recipe for Steamed Lamb Dumplings
(*Manty*) 1, and if you are using the butter place a small piece
on top.

Proceed as in recipe for Steamed Lamb Dumplings (*Manty*) 1.

Makes about 24 manty.

🍃 SMALL BOILED DUMPLINGS WITH LAMB
(Chuchvara)

DOUGH
2 cups flour
½ teaspoon salt
2 eggs
4–5 tablespoons water

FILLING
1 pound ground lamb
1 small onion, peeled and chopped
2 teaspoons water
1 teaspoon butter, softened
Salt and freshly ground black pepper

4 cups lamb or beef broth (optional)

Mix the flour and salt.

Beat the eggs with the water, and stir in the dry ingredients. Knead the dough until it forms a ball, and set it aside in a bowl for 1 hour, covered by a towel.

Combine the lamb, onion, water and butter, and add salt and pepper to taste.

Roll out the dough on a floured board to ¹⁄₁₆-inch thickness, and cut out small rounds 1½ inches in diameter.

Place 1 teaspoon of filling in the center of each round, cover with another round, and pinch the edges together tightly.

Drop the dumplings into the meat broth or into boiling salted water and simmer for 10–15 minutes, until they rise to the surface.

Makes about 30 chuchvara.
Serves 4.

These can be served in hot meat broth, or with sour cream, yogurt, melted butter or red wine vinegar on the side. The *chuchvara* can be sprinkled with cayenne pepper and with chopped fresh parsley, dill and coriander.

🦎 SMALL BOILED DUMPLINGS WITH POTATO
(*Kartoshka chuchvara*)

DOUGH
1 recipe for Small Lamb Boiled Dumplings (*Chuchvara*)
   dough (p. 174)

FILLING
1 large onion, peeled and finely chopped
4 tablespoons butter
3 medium potatoes, peeled and boiled
Salt and freshly ground black pepper

Make the dough as for Small Lamb Boiled Dumplings (*chuchvara*)

Fry the onion in the butter over medium-high heat for 10–15 minutes, until well browned, adding butter if needed. Mash the potatoes, and add salt and pepper to taste.

Combine the potatoes and onions, and mix well. Cool before filling the dumplings. Proceed as for Small Boiled Lamb Dumplings (*Chuchvara*).

Makes about 30 chuchvara.

Serve with melted butter, yogurt or sour cream on the side, sprinkled with cayenne pepper and fresh parsley and coriander to taste.

❧ SMALL BOILED DUMPLINGS WITH EGG
(Tukhum barak)

DOUGH
1 recipe for Small Lamb Boiled Dumplings (*Chuchvara*)
    dough (p. 174)

FILLING
6 hard-boiled eggs, peeled and cooled
4 scallions (green and white parts), finely minced
½ cup melted butter, cooled
Salt and freshly ground black pepper to taste

Chop hard-boiled eggs finely, and add the scallions.

Stir in the melted butter, being careful not to mash the eggs.

Add salt and pepper to taste.

Proceed as for Small Lamb Boiled Dumplings (*Chuchvara*).

Serves 4 (about 30 egg chuchvara).

Serve with sour cream or yogurt on the side, and sprinkle
with freshly ground black pepper or with cayenne pepper
to taste.

❧ LAMB SAMSAS 1

(Adapted from *Taste the World with Seattle's Sister Cities*: Kearney, NE: Morris Press, 1989)

DOUGH
1 egg + 1 egg yolk for egg wash
2 cups water
5½ cups flour (approximately)

FILLING
1¼ pounds lamb from shoulder, coarsely ground
1 large onion, peeled and finely chopped
1½ tablespoons cumin seeds, crushed
Salt and freshly ground black pepper

Put 1 egg, the water and 4 cups flour in a mixer and beat with dough hooks until a soft dough forms.

Keep adding flour (it will probably require about 1½ cups more) until the dough is malleable and does not stick do your hands.

Place the dough on a floured board and knead it for 3–4 minutes. Keep dough well covered.

Combine the lamb and onions; add the cumin and salt and pepper to taste.

Roll out one quarter of the dough on a floured board to ¼-inch thickness.

Cut out 4-inch rounds and place about 1½ teaspoons of filling in the center of each round. Do not heap in too much filling.

Pinch the opposite ends of the dough together tightly to form a round ball.

Continue until all the dough and filling are used up.

Preheat the oven to 350 degrees.

Beat the egg yolk well with 1 teaspoon water.

Place the *samsas* on a greased baking sheet and brush with the egg glaze.

Bake for 40–50 minutes or until golden.

Makes 3 dozen samsas.

🦁 LAMB SAMSAS 2

(Courtesy of Boris Elyukin and Elena Granovskiy)

DOUGH
1 pound packaged puff pastry

FILLING
1 recipe for filling for Steamed Lamb Dumplings
    (*Chuchvara*) 2 (p. 167), but omit the ¼ cup flour
    and ¼ cup water
1 egg yolk, beaten

Break off a piece of the puff pastry, and roll it in your hands to form a "sausage" about 1-inch thick. Break off pieces of the "sausage" about 1½-inches long.

Roll each out on a lightly floured board to ½-inch thickness, and cut each piece into a 4½ or 5-inch square.

Place 1½–2 tablespoons of filling in the center of each square and join the corners to form a triangle.

Preheat the oven to 325 degrees.

Place the filled *samsas* on a lightly greased baking sheet and brush them with the beaten egg yolk.

178

Bake at 325 degrees for 35–45 minutes, until golden brown.

Makes about 16 samsas.

🦁 SPICY MEAT SAMSAS

DOUGH
4 cups flour
Pinch salt
2 teaspoons baking powder
1¾ cups water
1 egg, well beaten + 1 egg yolk

FILLING
1¾ pounds beef or lamb, chopped into ¼-inch cubes
    or pea-size pieces
2 large onions, peeled and chopped
Salt to taste
1 teaspoon freshly ground black pepper
¼ teaspoon cayenne pepper
2 teaspoons butter

Mix the flour, salt and baking powder in a large bowl.

Beat the water with the egg and gradually add to the dry ingredients, beating well.

Work the dough until it can be handled easily, adding water if necessary.

Form the dough into a ball and set it aside in a bowl, covered by a towel, for 1 hour.

In a large bowl combine the meat, onions, salt, black and red pepper, and mix well with your hands.

Roll out the dough on a floured board to ¼-inch thickness, and cut out circles 4 to 4½ inches in diameter.

Place 2 tablespoons of filling in the center of each circle and fold up to form a round or triangular pastry. Place a tiny bit of butter on top of the filling. Pinch the edges tightly shut.

Preheat the oven to 375 degrees.

Beat the egg yolk with 1 teaspoon water and brush the *samsas* with the egg wash.

Place the *samsas* on a greased baking sheet and bake for 25–35 minutes at 375 degrees, until golden brown.

Makes about 2 dozen samsas.

❧ SAMSAS WITH MEAT-MUSHROOM FILLING
(Kuikorin samsa)

DOUGH

2 envelopes yeast
1½ cups water
1 teaspoon salt
1 egg + 1 teaspoon water for egg wash

FILLING
10 ounces mushrooms, washed
2 tablespoons vegetable oil
1 pound ground lamb
1 small onion, peeled and diced
Salt to taste
Pinch cayenne pepper
½ teaspoon powdered coriander
¼ cup chopped fresh coriander

In a medium-sized bowl sprinkle the yeast into 1 cup water, and add the salt. Stir well and allow to rest for 5 minutes.

Place the flour in a large bowl and gradually pour in the yeast mixture, stirring first with a wooden spoon and then with your hands.

Add the remaining ½ cup water (or a bit more, if needed) to form a fairly stiff dough that does not stick to your hands. Form the dough into a ball and knead it for 3–4 minutes.

Place the dough in a bowl, cover with a damp kitchen towel, and place in a warm place to rise for 50–60 minutes.

In the meantime, make the filling:

Remove any tough stems from the mushrooms and chop the mushrooms finely.

Heat the oil and stir in the meat and onions.

Break the mixture up with a wooden fork, and cook for 5–7 minutes until the meat has lost its red color and turned brown.

Add the mushrooms, salt to taste, cayenne, powdered and fresh coriander, and cook for another 3–4 minutes. Allow to cool.

Preheat the oven to 350 degrees.

Punch the dough down, pinch off a chunk the size of your fist, and roll it out on a lightly floured board to ¼-inch thickness, and cut out 4-inch squares. Keep remaining dough in the bowl with the damp towel covering it to prevent it from drying out.

Place 1 heaping teaspoon of filling in the center of each square and bring the opposite corners up towards each other to form a triangle.

Pinch the edges tightly shut.

Place the *samsas* on a greased baking sheet, being sure they do not touch.

Beat the egg and water together, and brush the tops of the *samsas* lightly with the egg wash. Let them sit at room temperature for 10–15 minutes, and then bake the *samsas* for 45–50 minutes, until golden brown and firm to the touch.

Makes about 4 dozen samsas.

These are good with cocktails or served with a chicken bouillon or light vegetable soup.

BEEF SAMSAS
(Parvoz samsa)

DOUGH
⅔ cup water
3 tablespoons butter, melted
3 eggs
½ teaspoon salt
3 cups flour

1 egg for glaze

FILLING
1¼ pounds beef for stew
1 large onion, peeled and cut into eighths
1 teaspoon ground cumin
Pinch cayenne pepper
Salt and freshly ground black pepper to taste

Combine the water, melted butter, 3 eggs and salt, and beat well.

Gradually sprinkle in the flour to form a medium stiff dough which no longer sticks to your hands.

Form a ball and allow the dough to rest for 40 minutes.

Cut the meat into ¼-inch cubes and finely chop the onion, or process the meat and onion in a food processor until the meat is just the size of small peas, but not until it looks like hamburger meat.

Add the cumin, cayenne, and salt and black pepper, and mix well.

Roll out the dough on a floured board and cut out circles 3 inches in diameter. Place 1 teaspoon of filling in the center of the dough and draw up the edges around the filling, pinching them together but leaving a small circle of filling exposed in the center.

Preheat the oven to 375 degrees. Place the *samsas* on a greased baking sheet. Beat the remaining egg and brush the *samsas* with the egg. Bake the *samsas* for 50 minutes or until dough is firm and golden brown. Loosen with a spatula, and serve hot.

Makes 40 samsas.

CABBAGE SAMSAS
(Karak samsa)

DOUGH
1 recipe dough for Spicy Meat *Samsas* (p. 179)

FILLING
6–8 tablespoons butter
2 small onions, peeled and finely chopped
½ small cabbage, shredded
Salt and freshly ground black pepper to taste
2 tablespoons tomato paste

Make dough as indicated for Spicy Meat *Samsas*.

Melt the butter and sauté the onions until soft but not brown.

Add the cabbage and sauté on medium low heat, stirring, until cabbage is soft, about 10 minutes. Add butter as needed.

Season with salt and pepper to taste.

Blend in the tomato paste.

Cool before filling the *samsas*.

Proceed as for Spicy Meat *Samsas*.

Makes about 2 dozen samsas.

 POTATO-ONION SAMSAS
(Kartoshkali kovurma baraki somsa)

DOUGH
1 recipe dough for Lamb *Samsas* (p. 177)

FILLING
3 large potatoes, peeled
2 large onions
5 tablespoons butter
Salt and freshly ground black pepper to taste

184

Boil the potatoes for about 6–8 minutes, until firm but not soft. Cut into very small (¼-inch) cubes.

Fry the onions in the butter until brown, about 10 minutes, adding butter if needed.

Mix in salt and pepper to taste.

Allow mixture to cool.

Proceed as for Lamb *Samsas*.

Makes about 3 dozen samsas.

EGG SAMSAS
(Tukhum samsa)

DOUGH
1 recipe for dough for *Samsas* with Meat-Mushroom Filling (p. 180)

FILLING
12 hard-boiled eggs, peeled, cooled and finely chopped
7 scallions (green part only), finely chopped
1 tablespoon chopped fresh dill
⅔ cup sour cream
Salt and pepper to taste

Combine the eggs, scallions and dill.

Stir in the sour cream by tablespoonfuls. Be careful not to mash the eggs. The mixture should not be thin; if your sour cream is runny, use less.

Season with salt and pepper to taste.

Proceed as for *Samsas* with Meat-Mushroom Filling.

Makes about 4 dozen samsas.

SQUASH SAMSAS
(Oshkovok samsa)

(Adapted from Darra Goldstein, *The Vegetarian Hearth*, Harper Collins, 1996)

SAMSA DOUGH
3 cups unbleached flour
1½ teaspoons salt, or to taste
1 cup warm water
2 tablespoons sour cream
1 egg yolk
1 teaspoon water

FILLING

6 tablespoons vegetable oil
2 large onions, peeled and minced
2 pounds butternut squash, peeled and grated,
    or yellow zucchini, trimmed and finely minced
½ teaspoon salt or to taste
½ teaspoon freshly ground black pepper
Pinch cayenne pepper
½ teaspoon ground cumin
½ teaspoon cumin seeds
½ teaspoon turmeric

Blend the flour and salt in a large bowl and make a well in the center.

Pour in the water, and knead until the dough no longer sticks to your hands.

Form it into a ball, cover with plastic wrap and allow to rise at room temperature for 1 hour.

Roll out the dough on a floured board into a large square.

Brush with the sour cream, roll up, and roll out into 2 long flat strips, about 2 inches in width.

Cover with plastic wrap and refrigerate for at least 2 hours.

In a frying pan heat 4 tablespoons of the oil and sauté the onion until soft but not brown.

Stir in the squash, salt, pepper, cayenne, cumin and turmeric, and simmer for 15 minutes, until a thick mass forms.

Cool thoroughly.

Roll out the dough to form 4-inch squares.

Place 1 heaping tablespoon of filling in the center of each square and bring up the corners to form a triangle.
Be sure the edges of the triangles are tightly pinched shut to prevent the filling from escaping.

Preheat the oven to 350 degrees.

Place the *samsas* on a well greased baking sheet.

Beat the egg yolk with 1 teaspoon water and brush the *samsas* with the glaze.

Bake for 20–25 minutes until firm and lightly browned.

Serve warm but not too hot. This is a good accompaniment to soups.

Makes 16–17 samsas.

❧ SQUASH OR PUMPKIN PASTRIES
(Bichak)

This Bukharan Jewish recipe is served on holidays such as Rosh Hashanah, the Jewish New Year. While traditionally made with pumpkin, they can also be made with squash, which is easier to find year-round.

DOUGH
1 envelope dry yeast
1 cup lukewarm water (approximately)
½ teaspoon sugar
4 cups unbleached flour
Pinch salt
1 egg yolk for glaze

SQUASH FILLING
1 pound coarsely chopped yellow zucchini) or 2 packages
    (8 ounces each) frozen yellow squash (do not use
    puréed squash), cooked and cooled
2 medium onions, peeled and finely chopped
2 tablespoons butter or margarine
Salt
Freshly ground black pepper

PUMPKIN FILLING:
1 small pumpkin, 2–3 pounds
2 large onions, peeled and finely chopped
6 tablespoons vegetable oil
Salt and freshly ground black pepper to taste
Pinch cayenne pepper
1 teaspoon powdered cumin

Dissolve the yeast in ½ cup of the water, add the sugar, and allow the mixture to stand for 10–12 minutes.

Combine the flour and salt, add the yeast mixture, and stir

188

in another half cup of water, or as much as is needed for the dough to form a ball.

Knead the dough on a floured board, adding a little more flour if needed.

Allow it to rise in a bowl covered with a damp towel, in a warm place such as a turned-off oven for 40–50 minutes.

Punch down the dough and cover with a damp towel to keep it moist.

FOR SQUASH FILLING:
Combine the squash with the onions.

Melt the butter in a shallow pan and add the squash and onions.

Cover and simmer over low heat for 15 minutes, stirring. Watch to see that the mixture does not burn, and add a little water if needed.

Drain well, add salt and pepper to taste, and chill until mixture has cooled completely.

FOR PUMPKIN FILLING:
Remove the pumpkin meat from the shell, and discard the seeds.

Grate the pumpkin flesh coarsely.

Sauté the onions in 3 tablespoons oil, stirring.

Add the salt, cayenne and cumin and stir, adding remaining oil as needed until the mixture holds together in a thick mass.

Cool the pumpkin filling thoroughly.

Preheat the oven to 375 degrees. Roll the dough out on a floured board to ¹⁄₁₆-inch thick, and cut out 4-inch squares.

Place 2 tablespoons of squash or pumpkin filling in the center of each round. Wet your fingers with cold water and pinch the ends to form triangles from the squares.

Mix the egg yolk with a teaspoon of water and beat lightly.

Place the dumplings on a greased baking sheet and brush with the egg yolk wash.

Bake at 375 degrees for 20–25 minutes, until the dumplings are golden brown.

Serves 6.
Makes about 20 stuffed pastries.

BAKED MEAT PIROZHKI
(Balishi)

DOUGH
1 envelope yeast
½ teaspoon sugar
½ teaspoon salt
¼ cup warm water
1 tablespoon melted butter, cooled
½ cup water (approximately)
2⅓ cups flour
1 egg for glaze
1 teaspoon water

FILLING
¾ pound ground lamb
½ small onion
Salt to taste
Freshly ground black pepper
½ teaspoon sweet paprika
½ teaspoon crushed cumin seeds
¼ teaspoon ground cumin

In a small bowl mix the yeast, sugar, salt and warm water, stirring until the yeast is completely dissolved. Set aside for 10 minutes.

Add the melted butter and stir.

Add the ½ cup water.

Put the flour into a large bowl, make a well in the center, and pour in the liquid.

Mix well and then knead with your hands until the dough forms a ball and no longer sticks to your hands.

Put it into a bowl, cover with a kitchen towel, and allow it to rise for 35 minutes.

In the meantime, make the filling by mixing the lamb with all the other ingredients for the filling.

When the dough has risen, punch it down and roll it out on a lightly floured board to form circles 3½ inches in diameter.

Place 1 teaspoon filling in the center of each round and bring up the edges on all sides to form a round *pirozhok*, leaving a small hole in the top center through which the filling is visible.

Place the *pirozhki* on a greased baking sheet and allow them to rise in a turned-off oven for 25 minutes.

Mix the egg with the teaspoon water and brush the *pirozhki* well with the egg glaze.

Preheat the oven to 425 degrees and bake the *pirozhki* for 10 minutes. Reduce the heat to 375 and bake for 20–25 more minutes, until they are golden brown and firm.

Makes 30 pirozhki.

❧ FRIED PIROZHKI
(Balishi)

These little meat pies are extremely moist and flavorful.

DOUGH
1 envelope yeast
½ cup warm water
1 teaspoon salt
1¼ cups unflavored yogurt
3¼ to 3¾ cups unbleached flour, sifted

FILLING
1 pound beef for stew, coarsely ground
1 large onion, peeled and finely chopped
Salt and freshly ground pepper to taste
Pinch cayenne pepper

1 cup vegetable oil for frying

In a large bowl combine the yeast, warm water and salt, and allow it to stand for 5 minutes.

Add the yogurt, and stir well.

Gradually blend in the flour, stirring and then kneading until a soft, elastic dough is formed which does not stick to your hands.

Form the dough into a ball, cover the bowl with a damp towel and allow it to rise in a warm place for 50 minutes.

Combine the beef, onion, salt, black and cayenne pepper, and mix well.

Punch the dough down and roll it out on a well floured board to ¼-inch thickness.

Cut into 4-inch rounds.

Place 1 teaspoon of filling in the center of each round and pull up the edges. Close the pastry on the top and flatten them slightly to form a flattened round pastry.

Allow the meat pies to rise for 30 minutes.

In a large, deep skillet heat the vegetable oil until it is very hot. Carefully lower 6 to 8 of the *pirozhki* into the oil. Be sure that they do not touch.

Fry over medium high heat for 5–6 minutes on each side, until they are a deep golden brown. Turn carefully with tongs.

Carefully remove the *pirozhki* from the oil with tongs and allow them to dry on paper towels.

Makes 3 dozen balishi.

Can be served with soup; these are very good with chicken broth or with a vegetable soup, or as a cocktail snack.

Keep hot in a 325-degree oven. If reheating, brush a little softened butter on the tops of the meat pies to keep the dough moist.

❦ EGG AND RICE FILLING FOR FRIED PIROZHKI
(Fried balishi)

1 recipe dough for Baked Meat Pirozhki (*Balishi*) (p. 190)
2 tablespoons butter + ¼ pound butter, softened
1 small onion, peeled and finely chopped
2 cups cooked rice
5 hard-boiled eggs, peeled and chopped
Salt and pepper to taste

Melt the 2 tablespoons butter in a small saucepan and fry the onion until golden brown, 7–9 minutes. Cool.

Combine the onion, rice, eggs, and salt and pepper to taste.

Work in the softened butter, taking care not to mash the eggs.

Roll out the *balishi* dough and proceed as for the meat *balishi*.

Makes 3 dozen balishi.

Can be served with a meat soup, with a green salad, or with cocktail snacks. The *balishi* can be kept warm in a 325-degree oven. When reheating, brush with a little softened butter to keep from drying out.

🌿 SAMSA GREEN SAUCE

(Courtesy of Lydia Barrett, Seattle)

¾ cup vegetable oil (do not use olive oil)
¼ cup lemon juice
½ teaspoon sugar
1 small clove garlic, minced
3 scallions, minced (green part only)
1 small Kirby cucumber, peeled and finely chopped
½ stalk celery, minced
¼ cup chopped fresh parsley
1 tablespoon chopped fresh dill

Blend the oil and lemon juice, and add the sugar and garlic, stirring to dissolve the sugar.

Blend together all the other ingredients, and combine with the oil mixture. Set the sauce aside at room temperature for 15 minutes.

Makes about 1½ cups sauce.

Serve on the side with *samsas*. This is also good as a salad dressing over fresh sliced tomatoes.

❧ YOGURT SAUCE

(For *Manty* and other Dumplings)

2 cups unflavored yogurt
3 medium cloves garlic, peeled and crushed
Salt
4 tablespoons chopped coriander or mint

Combine all the ingredients and stir to mix well. Chill for at least 6 hours.

Makes 2½ cups.

❧ SPICED WHITE VINEGAR

1 small sweet red pepper
2 cups white vinegar
1 large clove garlic, peeled and halved
½ small onion, peeled and cut into thin 1-inch pieces
5 sprigs fresh dill

Cut two 1-inch strips from the red pepper, and save the rest for another purpose.

Put the vinegar into a glass jar and add the garlic, onion, pepper and dill. Close the jar tightly, shake the contents well, and set it aside at room temperature for 1–2 days.

Strain and serve with liver or meat *shashlyk*, or with *manty*.

Makes 2 cups.

Note: You can leave the spices in the jar, as the mixture will look quite pretty on the table; in that case strain through a small sieve when serving.

❧ HOMEMADE LAGMAN NOODLES

(Adapted from Anya von Bremzen and John Welchman, *Please to the Table*: New York, Workman Publishing, 1990)

3½ cups all-purpose bleached flour
½ teaspoon salt
½ cup water
1 large egg, slightly beaten
2 tablespoons vegetable oil
Water
Salt

In a large bowl sift the flour and salt together.

Make a small well in the center and pour in the water, egg and oil.

Stir with a wooden spoon and then mix well with your hands until the dough is smooth.

On a floured board knead the dough for 5 minutes until it is elastic and does not stick to your hands.

Roll it out into a rectangle about ⅛-inch thick and trim the edges.

Roll the dough up loosely like a jelly roll, making sure it is not sticking to itself.

With a sharp knife cut the roll crosswise into thin strips to form the noodles.

Spread out the noodles on a large plate and dust lightly with flour.

Bring 2 quarts of salted water to a boil and add the noodles. Cook for about 5 minutes, until tender. Drain well.

Serves 6.

🌿 LAGMAN MEAT AND VEGETABLE STEW

Proceed as in Lagman Soup (p. 67), but reduce the broth to 6 cups.

Be careful to see that the stew does not burn, and add water if necessary.

Serves 4–5.

🌿 NOODLES WITH YOGURT
(Chup oshi)

FOR THE NOODLES
1 cup all-purpose unbleached flour
Pinch salt
1 egg
7 cups beef or lamb stock

Note: You can also use store-bought flat, thin egg noodles for this dish. Cook 2 cups of pasta for 5 to 6 minutes, until tender, and proceed with the sauce.

YOGURT SAUCE
1 medium onion, finely chopped
4 tablespoons butter
¼ cup yogurt
¼ cup sour cream
2 tablespoons buttermilk
Freshly ground black pepper
2 tablespoons chopped fresh parsley

TO MAKE THE NOODLES:
Sift the flour and salt together in a large bowl.

Make a well in the center and pour in the egg.

Stir with a spoon and then work the dough with your hands until smooth, adding a few teaspoons water if necessary. Form the dough into a ball, place it in a lightly floured bowl, cover with a towel and set it aside for 25 minutes.

Roll out the dough on a floured board to ⅛-inch thickness, turning it over several times. Allow the dough to rest again for 1 to 2 hours.

Roll up the dough loosely into a jelly roll and cut it into thin strips. Let the strips dry out on a towel for 2 to 3 hours.

Bring the stock to a boil and drop in the noodles; cook for about 8 minutes, until tender.

Drain well before combining with sauce.

TO MAKE THE SAUCE:
Melt the butter and sauté the onions on low to medium heat until golden, about 5 to 7 minutes. Do not brown.

Combine the yogurt, sour cream and buttermilk, and stir into the onion, but do not bring the mixture to a boil.

Add the noodles, sprinkle with pepper and reheat until warm. Sprinkle with parsley just before serving.

Serves 4.

❧ STEAMED MEAT ROLL
(Guishtli khunon)

DOUGH
1 cup + 1 tablespoon flour
1 teaspoon salt
2 eggs
2 tablespoons water
2 tablespoons softened butter or margarine

FILLING
¼ pound beef or lamb for stew
1 small onion, peeled and coarsely chopped
1 small potato, peeled and coarsely chopped
Salt and freshly ground pepper to taste

Mix the flour and salt in a large bowl.

Combine the eggs and water and beat well.

Make a well in the center of the flour and pour in the egg mixture.

Mix well until a fairly stiff dough forms.

Knead the dough until smooth, form it into a ball and set it aside in a bowl, covered, for 30 minutes.

In the meantime, make the filling. Put the lamb, onion, potato, salt and pepper in a food processor and process for a few seconds until the mixture forms small pieces the size of peas or large crumbs. Do not overprocess or purée.

Roll out the dough on a lightly floured board to ¼-inch thickness to form a rectangle approximately 10 x 15 inches in size. Smear the dough evenly with the softened butter or margarine.

Place the filling on the dough in a thin, even layer, leaving 1 inch free on all sides.

Roll up the dough roll lengthwise to form a long thick "sausage."

Pinch the ends shut, and pinch the seam to close it well.

Place the roll, curving it slightly to fit into the steamer, onto a lightly greased steamer and steam, tightly covered, for 30-40 minutes.

Cut crosswise into pieces to serve.

Serves 6.

This meat roll is usually served with fresh tomatoes, tomato sauce, and fried onion rings. A barbecue sauce or even ketchup also goes quite well with the dish. Sautéed baby carrots, creamed spinach or steamed broccoli are good accompaniments. To reheat the roll brush it with a little softened butter or margarine to keep the noodle dough moist.

❧ STEAMED NOODLE STEW
(Dimlama lagman)

4 tablespoons vegetable oil
1 medium onion, peeled and finely chopped
3 whole cloves garlic, peeled and halved
½ pound ground beef
2 medium carrots, peeled and cut into thin julienne strips
1 small sweet green Italian pepper, trimmed, seeded and cut
    into thin rings
1 can (15 ounces) crushed tomatoes.
1 small eggplant, peeled, seeded and cut into 1-inch cubes
1 medium potato, peeled and cut into 1-inch cubes
1½ cups chopped cabbage
½ cup white radish, cut into thin julienne strips
Salt and freshly ground black pepper to taste
1 bay leaf
½ teaspoon ground cumin
½ teaspoon ground coriander
2 cups egg noodles, cooked *al dente*

Heat the oil in a large flame-proof casserole or Dutch oven, and sauté the onion and garlic for 3–4 minutes over medium heat.

Add the ground beef and cook, stirring, until meat is lightly browned.

Stir in the carrots, green pepper, tomatoes and eggplant, and blend.

Cover the pot and simmer over medium heat for 20 minutes, checking to see that there is enough liquid; if the stew starts to burn, add a little water.

Add the potato, cabbage, and white radish. Stir well and pour in enough water to just cover the mixture.

Stir in the salt, pepper, bay leaf, cumin and coriander, and bring the mixture to a boil.

Reduce the heat, cover the pot, and simmer on low heat for 30 minutes, until all the vegetables are very tender.

Drain the noodles well and place them on top of the meat and vegetable mixture, adding water if needed.

Cover the pot and simmer for another 10 minutes.

Taste for seasoning and adjust salt and pepper as needed.

Place a serving of noodles in each bowl and cover with the meat and vegetable stew.

Serves 6.

Serve with freshly ground black pepper and red wine vinegar on the side.

FRIED LAGMAN
(Kovurma lagman)

2 cups home-made lagman or store-bought thin
flat egg noodles
2 tablespoons butter, softened
4 tablespoons vegetable oil
2 medium onions, peeled and finely chopped
1½ pounds lamb, cut from the shoulder, cut into
¼-inch cubes or chopped into pea-sized pieces
in a food processor
1 can (1 pound) whole tomatoes, drained and crushed
3 tablespoons tomato paste
2 cloves garlic, peeled and crushed
Salt and pepper
2 eggs
1 tablespoon butter
2 tablespoons chopped fresh parsley
2 tablespoons chopped fresh dill

Cook the noodles in boiling water for 4 minutes, until they soften but are not cooked through.

Drain well, and in a large bowl gently mix in the 2 tablespoons softened butter.

Heat the vegetable oil, add the onions, and cook until golden.

Add the meat and brown well on all sides.

Stir in the tomatoes, tomato paste, and garlic.

Add salt and pepper to taste, cover, and cook for 20 minutes on low heat.

Beat the eggs well, and add salt to taste.

In a small frying pan melt the 1 tablespoon butter and cook the eggs to form an omelet, turning it once.

Cut the omelet into small strips ½-inch wide and about 1-inch long.

Add the omelet strips to the noodle mixture and cook for another 5 minutes.

Taste for seasoning, and sprinkle with the parsley and dill.

Serves 5.

🦎 NOODLES WITH EGG
(Tukhum lagman)

3 tablespoons vegetable oil
1 medium onion, peeled and cut into semicircular rings
2 whole cloves garlic, peeled
¾ pound ground beef or lamb
½ cup grated white radish (daikon)
2 tablespoons tomato paste
1 cup beef or lamb broth
Salt and pepper to taste
2 tablespoons butter
2 cups cooked egg noodles
3 eggs, well beaten
1 tablespoon chopped fresh parsley
1 tablespoon chopped fresh coriander

Heat the oil and sauté the onion over medium high heat until golden, about 5–7 minutes.

Add the garlic, ground meat, and white radish, and cook, stirring, until meat is lightly browned. Add a little more oil if needed to keep the meat from burning.

Stir in the tomato paste and meat broth, cover the pot, and cook on medium low heat for 20 minutes. If the meat starts to burn, add a little more broth or water.

Season to taste with salt and pepper.

In a separate frying pan melt the butter and gently toss the noodles for a few minutes over medium-low heat.

Pour the eggs over the noodles and cook, stirring gently, until the eggs are set.

Transfer the noodles and eggs to the pan with the meat and stir until blended.

Sprinkle with the parsley and coriander just before serving.

Serves 4–5.

Serve with freshly ground black pepper and red wine vinegar on the side. Flatbread or French bread to absorb the sauce is a good accompaniment, along with a green salad.

MEAT PANCAKES
(Kiimali blinchiki)

PANCAKES
4 eggs
1 cup flour
½ teaspoon salt
½ teaspoon baking soda
1 cup milk
2 teaspoons butter + extra butter for frying

FILLING
2 tablespoons vegetable oil
1 medium onion, peeled and finely chopped
1 pound beef or lamb, coarsely ground
1 hard-boiled egg, peeled and chopped
Salt and freshly ground pepper to taste
1 tablespoon chopped fresh parsley

Beat the eggs well.

Combine the flour, salt, and baking soda in a large bowl.

Make a well in the center and pour in the eggs; stir to mix.

Add the milk and beat until blended.

Melt 1 teaspoon butter and add to the batter.

Heat the vegetable oil and fry the onion over medium heat until golden.

Add the onion, meat, chopped eggs, salt and pepper, and cook until meat is well browned. Remove from heat and stir in the parsley.

Melt the remaining teaspoon butter in a small (6-inch) skillet.

Pour in ½ soup ladle of batter and cook for a few minutes until light brown on bottom. Remove to a clean towel; do not fry it on the other side.

Continue until all of the batter has been used up, putting layers of wax paper between the pancakes to keep them from sticking to each other. Add extra butter for frying as needed.

Place 1 heaping tablespoon of filling in the center of each pancake and roll up.

Makes 16–20 pancakes.

Serve with sour cream or red wine vinegar on the side. You can keep the pancakes warm in a lightly greased baking dish at 325 degrees.

🦔 PUFFY SMALL PANCAKES
(Kuimok)

¾ cup milk
Pinch salt
2 teaspoons sugar
1 cup flour
2 teaspoons baking soda
2 eggs
Butter for frying

In a medium-sized bowl combine the milk, salt and sugar.

Combine the flour and baking soda, and beat into the milk mixture.

Add the eggs, and beat with a whisk until blended.

In a small (6 to 7-inch) frying pan heat a teaspoon of butter until very hot.

Pour in a ladleful of batter (diameter of the pancake should be no more than 4 inches).

Fry quickly on medium high heat on both sides, adding butter as needed.

Keep hot in a 325-degree oven, if needed.

Makes about 12–14 pancakes.

These pancakes can be served with jam and sour cream as an accompaniment to tea, or with melted butter, red caviar and smoked salmon or whitefish as an appetizer or lunch dish.

🌿 SCALLION PANCAKES
(Galmana)

1½ cups flour
1 teaspoon salt
⅔ cup water
½ cup sour cream (approximately)
8 scallions, minced (green part only)
Vegetable oil for frying (about ⅔ cup)

Combine the flour and salt and blend in the water, kneading to form a dough which does not stick to your hands; add more flour as needed.

Set the dough aside, covered, for 15 minutes.

Roll out the dough on a floured board with a floured rolling pin to ¼-inch thickness.

Cut out 5-inch squares.

Brush each square thickly with the sour cream, using a pastry brush.

Sprinkle each square with some of the scallions, and fold the top half over to form a rectangle. You do not need to pinch the edges tightly shut; pat the rectangle lightly to close.

Heat the oil until it is very hot and carefully lower in the scallion pancakes.

Fry for a few minutes on each side until stiff and golden brown.

Dry the pancakes between paper towels for a few minutes.

If not serving immediately, keep hot in a warm (325-degree) oven.

Makes 8 scallion pancakes.

These are a good accompaniment to a meat soup or stew.

VEGETABLES

Eggplant, pumpkin, squash, tomatoes, beans, cabbage, potatoes and chickpeas all abound in Uzbek recipes. The national dish of onions and carrots, *Sabzi piez*, comes in numerous variations. Vegetables are boiled, steamed, braised or fried, and tend to be thoroughly cooked rather than blanched or briefly sautéed. There are many recipes for stuffed vegetables such as peppers, onions or turnips. Mung beans and rice are combined with different ingredients to produce a variety of slow-simmered stews which form a dish in themselves or accompany main courses. Vegetables stews, *dimlama*, consist of ingredients simmered slowly in their own juices, producing dishes with virtually no fat.

🌿 VEGETABLE STEW
(Dimlama)

4 tablespoons vegetable oil
2 large onions, peeled and coarsely chopped
2 medium carrots, peeled and coarsely cubed
1 medium turnip, peeled and coarsely chopped
1 small sweet Italian pepper, trimmed, seeded,
    and coarsely chopped
2 medium yellow zucchini, trimmed and coarsely chopped
1 small eggplant, peeled and diced
1 can (15 ounces) crushed tomatoes
Salt and freshly ground black pepper
Pinch cayenne pepper
½ teaspoon cumin seeds
½ teaspoon ground cumin
2 tablespoons chopped fresh parsley
2 tablespoons chopped fresh coriander

Heat the oil in a heavy pot and sauté the onion in it for a few minutes, until soft but not brown.

Add the carrots, turnip, pepper, zucchini, and eggplant, and sauté for a few minutes.

Stir in the tomatoes, salt, pepper, cayenne and cumin, and mix well over low heat.

Cover the pot and cook on low heat for 50 minutes, until the vegetables are all very tender.

Sprinkle with the parsley and coriander just before serving.

Serves 6.

The vegetable stew can be served over noodles or rice, or as an accompaniment to meat or chicken dishes.

🌿 BRAISED VEGETABLE AND FRUIT STEW
(Meva va sabzavot dimlamasi)

2 tablespoons vegetable oil
1 medium onion, peeled and cut into semicircular rings
2 carrots, peeled and coarsely cubed
2 large tomatoes, coarsely chopped
2 medium potatoes, peeled and diced
1 small sweet Italian pepper, trimmed and seeded
Salt
¼ cup + 2 tablespoons chopped fresh parsley
¼ cup + 2 tablespoons chopped fresh coriander
1 large quince, peeled, cored and coarsely chopped
1 tart apple, peeled, cored and coarsely chopped
2 cups (approximately) chicken broth (or water,
     if you want a vegetarian dish)

Heat the oil in a heavy pot and sauté the onion in it for a few minutes, until soft but not brown.

Add the carrots, tomatoes, potatoes, sweet pepper, salt to taste, ¼ cup parsley and ¼ cup coriander, and mix well over low heat.

Add the chopped quince and apple, stirring to blend, and pour in just enough broth to cover the mixture.

Cover the pot and braise over low heat for 45 minutes; add water or broth if needed to keep the stew from burning.

Sprinkle with the remaining parsley and coriander just before serving.

Serves 4.

The stew can be served over noodles or rice, or as an accompaniment to grilled chicken or meat dishes.

❧ MUNG BEAN STEW
(Mashkitchiri)

¼ cup vegetable oil
1 medium onion, finely chopped
1 large carrot, peeled and diced
1 large potato, peeled and cubed
2 large ripe tomatoes, peeled and coarsely chopped
1 teaspoon cumin seeds
½ teaspoon hot Hungarian paprika
Salt and pepper
4½ cups boiling chicken stock (or water, if you want
      a vegetarian dish), divided
¾ cup mung beans, soaked overnight in salted water to
      cover, and well drained
1 cup rice
2 tablespoons chopped fresh coriander

Heat the oil until it starts to smoke and sauté the onions until they begin to turn golden, about 5 minutes.

Add the carrots and potato and cook until they start to brown, about 10 minutes.

Mix in the tomatoes, cumin, paprika, and salt and pepper to taste.

Add 1½ cups of boiling stock and let the mixture boil for 5 minutes.

Stir in the mung beans, reduce the heat, cover, and cook on low heat for about 40 minutes, until the beans are tender.

Place the remaining 3 cups boiling stock or water in a medium-sized pot and stir in the rice. Boil the rice for two minutes, reduce the heat to low, cover the pot, and cook for about 20 minutes, until all the liquid is absorbed and the rice is tender.

Stir the rice into the vegetable mixture, sprinkle with coriander, and serve.

Serves 6.

🌿 RICE AND MUNG BEANS
(*Mashkitchiri 2*)

6 cups water
1½ cups mung beans
1 cup rice
Salt and freshly ground black pepper
1 cup yogurt
2 tablespoons chopped fresh coriander
1 clove garlic, minced

Put the water in a pot and add the mung beans, rice, salt and pepper.

Bring to a boil.

Cover the pot and simmer over low heat for 1 hour, until the rice and beans are very soft, checking that there is enough liquid and that the mixture does not burn. By the end of the cooking period the liquid should have entirely evaporated.

Combine the yogurt, salt, coriander and garlic.

Drain off any extra liquid from the rice and bean mixture, and cool slightly.

Add the yogurt sauce and stir.

Serves 6.

🦎 SPICY CARROTS AND ONIONS
(Sabzi piez)

3 tablespoons butter
2 medium onions, peeled and thinly sliced
4 large carrots, peeled and cut into julienne,
     1½ inches × ¼ inch
1 large tomato, peeled, seeded and chopped
2 teaspoons tomato paste
Salt to taste
⅛ teaspoon cayenne pepper
1 teaspoon cumin seeds
2 whole cloves garlic, unpeeled
¼–½ cup water or beef broth
¼ cup scallions, chopped (white and green parts)

Heat the butter in a large, heavy skillet.

Add the onions and cook, stirring, on moderate heat, for about 6–8 minutes, until they are golden.

Add the carrots, and cook for another few minutes.

Stir in the tomatoes and tomato paste, raise the heat, and cook, stirring, for a few minutes until most of the liquid from the tomatoes has disappeared.

Add salt to taste, the cayenne, cumin, and garlic, and enough water or beef broth to just cover the vegetables.

Reduce the heat and simmer, covered for about 10 minutes, until the carrots are tender and the liquid has reduced, about 20 minutes.

Discard the garlic, and sprinkle with the scallions just before serving.

Serves 5.

🦁 SPICED CHICKPEAS
(Nukhakhurak)

1 pound dried chickpeas, soaked in cold water overnight
2 medium onions, peeled and coarsely chopped
2 medium carrots, peeled and coarsely chopped
Salt
Pinch cayenne pepper
1 teaspoon cumin seeds
2 teaspoons red wine vinegar
2 scallions, minced (green and white parts)

Drain the chickpeas well, and place in a pot with the onions and carrots.

Pour in water to cover the vegetables by 2 inches.

Add salt to taste, the cayenne, the cumin and vinegar, and bring to a boil.

Reduce the heat, cover, and cook on low heat for 50 minutes, or until the chickpeas are very soft.

Drain well. Taste for seasoning and add salt and cayenne as needed.

Sprinkle with scallions just before serving.

Serves 4–6.

🌿 BEANS WITH GARLIC
(Kainatma lovia)

1 pound white beans, soaked in cold water overnight
1 large onion, peeled and diced
2 large carrots, peeled and diced
3 large cloves garlic, peeled and coarsely sliced
Salt
2 tablespoons butter, melted

Drain the beans well. Place them in a pot with water covering them by 2 inches, and add the onion, carrots, garlic and salt.

Cook on medium high heat for 30 minutes, checking to be sure there is enough water, until the beans are soft.

Drain well, and taste for seasoning, adding salt as needed.

Blend in the melted butter, taking care not to crush the beans.

Serves 4–6.

This goes well with lamb dishes.

🌿 POTATOES AND ONIONS
(Kartoshka biiron)

3 tablespoons vegetable oil
2 medium onions, peeled and cut into semicircular rings
3 medium potatoes, peeled and cut into ¼-inch rounds
Salt
1 tablespoon chopped fresh dill
1 tablespoon chopped fresh parsley

Heat the oil in a large frying pan and fry the onions until golden, 5–7 minutes.

Add the potato slices, sprinkle with salt, and fry on medium high heat for about 5–8 minutes, until the potatoes are crisp and golden. Add oil if needed.

Pour in just enough water to cover the potatoes and onions, and bring to a boil.

Reduce the heat, cover the pan, and cook on low heat for 8–12 minutes, until potatoes are cooked through.

Sprinkle with the chopped dill and parsley just before serving.

Serves 4.

🌿 POTATO AND ONION OMELET
(*Kartoshka kuimok*)

4 eggs
Salt
2 tablespoons chopped fresh parsley
2 tablespoons chopped fresh coriander
2 tablespoons butter
1 medium onion, peeled and cut into thin semicircular
    rings
1 medium potato, peeled and cut into very thin strips
    (1 inch × ¼ inch)

Beat the eggs well and add salt to taste.

Blend in 1 tablespoon of the parsley, and 1 tablespoon of the coriander.

Melt the butter and sauté the onion for a few minutes until soft.

Add the potato strips, and fry until strips begin to become crisp. Add more butter if needed.

Pour in the eggs and sprinkle with a little additional salt, if desired.

Cook over medium low heat until eggs are set.

Sprinkle with remaining parsley and coriander, and serve.

Serves 2–3.

🦐 BRAISED CAULIFLOWER
(*Gulkaram biiron*)

½ large cauliflower, washed and cut into small florets
2 tablespoons butter
1 small onion, peeled and finely chopped
4 tablespoons beef gravy drippings or beef broth
Salt and pepper
2 tablespoons chopped fresh parsley
1 tablespoon chopped fresh coriander

Cook the cauliflower in boiling salted water (enough to cover the florets) for 6–8 minutes, until softened but not completely cooked, and drain.

Meanwhile, melt 1 tablespoon butter over medium high heat, add the onion and cook, stirring, until onion starts to turn golden brown.

Stir in the drained cauliflower, lower the heat, and pour in the beef broth.

Add the remaining 1 tablespoon butter and mix over low heat.

Sprinkle with salt and pepper to taste.

Cook, covered, over low heat for 5–7 minutes more.

Just before serving sprinkle with the parsley and coriander, and stir well.

Serves 4.

🌿 FRIED MUSHROOMS
(Kuizikorin kovurma)

2½ pounds mushrooms
Salt
3 medium onions, peeled
½ cup vegetable oil or 8 tablespoons butter, melted
½ cup strong beef broth
½ cup chopped fresh coriander

Wash the mushrooms well and chop them very coarsely. If they are small, cut them in half.

Fill a large bowl with cold water, add about 2 teaspoons salt, and soak the mushrooms in the salted water for 2–3 minutes.

Drain well.

Chop the onions finely.

Heat the oil or butter, add the mushrooms and onions, and stir well over medium high heat.

Cook for 7–8 minutes until the onions are soft and the mushrooms give off a lot of their liquid.

Lower the heat if necessary to keep the mixture from burning.

Salt lightly and add the beef broth. Bring the mixture to a boil, stirring well.

Reduce the heat, cover, and simmer for 10 minutes.

Just before serving stir in the coriander.

Serves 6–8 as a side dish.

Since the mushrooms will have plenty of sauce, this dish is good with *plovs* or noodle dishes which can absorb the liquid.

🦎 GRILLED TOMATOES
(Pomidori kovurma)

6 small tomatoes
6 small onions, peeled and quartered
Vegetable oil
Salt
Cayenne pepper

Wash the tomatoes and onions and pat dry.

Thread the tomatoes and onions on a skewer so that the vegetables do not touch each other.

Coat very lightly with vegetable oil.

Grill over hot coals or in a broiler for a few minutes, turning once, and checking to see that they do not burn.

Remove the tomatoes from the skewers and carefully immerse them for a few seconds in hot salt water.

Sprinkle with salt and with cayenne to taste.

Serve on a platter surrounded by the onions.

Note: This is often served with *shashlyk*. In that case you can grill the whole onions on the skewers, alternating them with the tomatoes, but do not immerse the onions in salt water.

Serves 4–6.

🌺 MARINATED TOMATOES
(*Khavasga tuzlangan pomidor*)

2 ripe, fairly large tomatoes
Salt
2 tablespoons vegetable oil
½ medium onion, peeled and finely chopped
2 tablespoons finely chopped fresh coriander
2 tablespoons finely chopped fresh Italian flat-leaf parsley
1 tablespoon chopped fresh dill
1 small clove garlic, peeled and finely chopped (optional)

Carefully trim the tops of the tomatoes, and cut the tomatoes across the center but not all the way, leaving the two halves joined in the middle.

Scoop out about ⅔ of the pulp, being sure not to tear the shell.

Sprinkle the halves generously with salt.

Heat the oil and fry the onion until golden brown, about 5 minutes. Allow it to cool slightly.

Off heat, add the coriander, parsley, dill and the garlic (if you are using it) to the onion, and mix well.

Pack the mixture into the joined tomato halves, and close the halves.

Place the tomatoes in a small dish and put a plate with a weight on it over them. (A small casserole or 2–3 soup cans are fine.)

Refrigerate overnight. (If you don't have time to leave them overnight leave the dish at room temperature for 1 hour and then chill for 1 more hour.)

Pour off any excess oil, and carefully separate the tomato halves. They should be served at room temperature.

Makes 4 halves.

These tomatoes are a particularly good accompaniment to *shashlyk* or grilled chicken.

🌿 TOMATOES WITH EGGS
(Pomidor kuimok)

2 large tomatoes
1 teaspoon butter
2 eggs
Salt
2 teaspoons chopped fresh coriander

Wash the tomatoes, cut a thin slice off the top, and scoop out the flesh and seeds, taking care not to pierce through the shell.

Dot the inside of each tomato shell with ½ teaspoon butter.

Beat the eggs well, adding salt to taste.

Set the tomatoes in a buttered oven-proof casserole, and carefully pour the eggs into the shell.

Cook under the broiler for about 5–6 minutes, watching carefully to see that the eggs do not burn. (Note: Do not bake the eggs in the oven. It will take a very long time for the eggs to cook properly, and the tomato shells will soften and start to collapse before the eggs are done).

If you need to wait before serving, place the casserole in a 300-degree oven. Just before serving sprinkle with the chopped coriander.

Serves 2.

Note: The number of eggs you will need will depend on their size and on the size of the tomatoes.

✤ STUFFED TOMATOES
(Pomidor duilma)

Prepare as for stuffed peppers, using 6 large tomatoes instead of the peppers. If the tomatoes are small the vegetables will cook faster, about 35–45 minutes.

Serves 6.

✤ STUFFED PEPPERS
(Bolgari duilma)

6 medium bell peppers
1 pound coarsely ground beef or lamb
2 medium onions, peeled and finely chopped
2 small carrots, peeled and finely chopped
3 tablespoons cooked rice
Salt and freshly ground black pepper
Pinch cayenne pepper
½ teaspoon ground cumin
¼ teaspoon sweet paprika
3 tablespoons vegetable oil
1 tablespoon tomato paste
2½ to 3½ cups meat broth
1 bay leaf

Carefully remove the seeds and ribs of the peppers, taking care not to break the shells.

Combine 1 onion, 1 carrot, 3 tablespoons rice, salt, black pepper, cayenne, ground cumin and paprika with the ground meat.

Stuff the pepper shells with the meat mixture.

Heat the oil in a flame-proof casserole or Dutch oven and sauté the remaining onion and carrot in it for a few minutes, until soft.

Add the tomato paste, and mix well.

Pour in 2½ cups meat broth and stir well.

Add the bay leaf.

Put the stuffed pepper shells on top of the vegetable mixture and bring the pot to a boil.

Reduce the heat, cover, and simmer for 45–50 minutes, checking to see that there is enough liquid so that the peppers do not burn. Add more broth or water if needed.

Remove the bay leaf.

Serves 6.

Serve with yogurt or sour cream on the side.

🥬 STUFFED EGGPLANT
(Sazevot duilma)

4 medium eggplants
⅓ cup vegetable oil (approximately)
1 pound coarsely ground beef or lamb
1 large onion, peeled and finely chopped
2 tablespoons tomato paste
½ cup cooked rice
Salt and freshly ground black pepper
1 tablespoon chopped fresh dill
Sour cream

Cut the eggplants in half and remove the seeds and about 6–8 tablespoons of flesh from the center of each one, leaving a very thick shell.

Dice the eggplant pulp finely. Heat the oil and and sauté the eggplant for 10 minutes until the pieces soften, adding more oil if needed.

Mix the ground meat, onion, tomato paste, rice, salt, pepper and dill.

Stuff the eggplant shells with the meat mixture.

Preheat the oven to 350 degrees.

Place the eggplants in a lightly buttered baking dish and pour about 1 inch of water on the bottom.

Bake for 45–50 minutes until eggplants are soft and the filling is cooked through. If they start to dry out put a little more water in the baking pan.

Serves 8.

🦎 STUFFED ONIONS
(Piez duilma)

4 large onions
1 medium carrot, peeled and shredded
½ cup celery, finely diced
1 small clove garlic, peeled and minced
Salt and freshly ground black pepper
½ teaspoon ground cumin
¼ teaspoon cumin seeds
½ pound ground lamb or beef
1 small egg, beaten
2 tablespoons cooked rice
3 tablespoons vegetable oil
1 tablespoon tomato paste
½ teaspoon lemon juice
⅓ cup cooked chickpeas
⅓ cup diced yellow zucchini
2 cups beef or lamb broth

Parboil the onions (whole) in water to cover for 2 minutes on medium heat.

Remove the onions, and peel off 2–3 of the tough outer layers. Carefully remove and reserve the onion pulp, leaving a thick shell.

Combine the carrot, celery, garlic, salt, pepper, ground cumin and cumin seeds with the ground meat.

Blend in the egg, and then the rice.

Stuff the onion shells with the meat mixture.

Heat the oil and sauté the onion pulp in it for a few minutes, until soft. Add the tomato paste, lemon juice, chickpeas and zucchini, and stir.

Pour in the meat broth and stir well.

Put the onion shells in the pot and bring the pot to a boil.

Reduce the heat, cover the pot, and simmer for 50–55 minutes, checking to see that there is enough liquid that the onions do not burn.

Serves 4.

🌿 STUFFED TURNIPS
(Shalgam duilma)

6 medium turnips
1 small carrot, peeled and finely chopped
1 small onion, peeled and finely chopped
½ pound ground lamb or beef
2 tablespoons cooked rice
1 egg
Salt and freshly ground pepper
Sour cream or yogurt

Peel the turnips and hollow out the flesh to form thick shells. Be careful not to tear the shells.

Dice the turnip flesh finely, and mix with the carrot, onion, and ground meat.

Add the rice, egg, and salt and pepper to taste.

Stuff the turnip shells with the mixture, and steam, covered, for 35–40 minutes, until the turnips are soft and the meat is cooked through.

Serves 6.

Serve with sour cream or yogurt on the side.

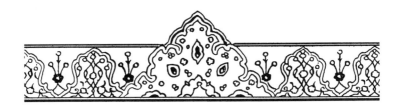

BREADS

Bread plays an enormously important role in Uzbek cuisine, and the flatbreads, *non*, are a part of almost every meal. The first foods that catch your eye at an Uzbek market are the piles of round onion, cumin, sesame and poppy seed breads stamped with all kinds of decorative patterns, fragrant and fresh from the oven. Before dinner is served in an Uzbek home the host breaks off pieces from a freshly baked loaf and passes them to all the guests, a ritual of communal "breaking bread" which precedes all the other courses. While the flat *non* is similar to the flatbreads of India and the thin pitas of the Middle East, there are also yeast breads and puffy buns. The steamed coriander buns show a strong Chinese influence.

The amount of flour needed may vary somewhat, depending on the type of flour you are using. The dough should be malleable and not stick to your hands.

🌿 GARLIC AND ONION WHOLEWHEAT
YEAST FLATBREAD
(Non)

2½ cups lukewarm water (105–115 degrees)
1 envelope active dry yeast
1½ teaspoons sugar
1 tablespoon vegetable oil
⅔ teaspoon salt
4–4½ cups unbleached all-purpose white flour
2 cups wholewheat flour
Butter (about ¼ cup)
2 medium onions, peeled and finely minced
1 teaspoon minced garlic

In a large bowl stir together ¼ cup water, yeast, and sugar, and let it stand 5 minutes.

Add the remaining water, oil and salt, and, a cup at a time, 4 cups of the all-purpose white flour and all the wholewheat flour.

Blend well after each addition.

Place the dough on a floured board and knead until the dough is smooth and does not stick to your hands, adding the additional white flour if needed to prevent sticking.

Form the dough into a ball, place it in a buttered bowl and turn it so that all sides are coated with butter.

Cover with a light kitchen towel and allow to rise until the dough doubles in size, about 1½ hours.

Divide the dough into 8 pieces and shape each into a ball.

On a floured board roll out each ball with a floured rolling pin into a circle about 7 inches in diameter.

Brush each round with cold water.

Cover again with the towel and allow to stand for 30 minutes.

Preheat the oven to 500 degrees, and heat a heavy baking sheet in the oven for 15 minutes.

While it is heating, wet your hands and make a 2-inch round indentation in the center of each circle of dough.

Prick all over the inner circle with a fork in a circular pattern.

Sprinkle the center of the breads with the onion and garlic.

Carefully remove the hot baking sheet from the oven.

Sprinkle each round lightly with cold water and place it on the sheet.

Bake in the lowest part of the oven for 12–15 minutes, until the dough is golden and has baked through.

Remove from the oven and set the breads aside for 15 minutes before serving.

Makes 8 breads.

❧ ONION FLATBREAD
(Non)

6 tablespoons butter
2 medium onions, very finely chopped
¾ cup warm water (110–115 degrees)
1 teaspoon salt
3 cups all-purpose unbleached flour

In a large heavy skillet melt 1 tablespoon of butter, and add the onions.

Cook, stirring, over low heat until the onions are soft and transparent, but not brown.

Remove them to a bowl and allow to cool.

In the same skillet, melt the remaining butter and then place it in a large bowl.

Add the warm water, and stir in the salt and onions.

Sprinkle in the flour, about one half a cup at a time, until the dough does not stick to the hands.

This may take a bit more or less than 3 cups of flour.

Knead the dough slightly, cover it with a towel and set it aside for 20 minutes.

Form about 10–12 balls from the dough, each about 2 inches in diameter.

On a lightly floured board roll out each ball into a flat circle about 7–8 inches in diameter.

Heat an ungreased pan (teflon will do this nicely) over high heat and brown each dough circle for a few (3–4) minutes on each side, turning the breads with a pancake turner or wide spatula. They will not brown evenly.

Allow the breads to dry on a rack. If needed, place them on an ungreased cookie sheet to crisp them and bake them for 5 minutes in a 250-degree oven.

Makes about 10–12 breads.

🌿 UZBEK FLATBREAD
(Non)

(Courtesy of Isak Barayev, Uzbek Tandoori Bakery, Queens, New York)

2½ cups lukewarm water
1 envelope dry yeast
2 teaspoons sugar
Salt to taste (preferably at least 2 teaspoons)
6½ cups flour
Butter (about ¼ cup)
2 teaspoons white sesame seeds
2 teaspoons black sesame seeds or nigella

In a large bowl or in a mixer with a dough hook blend ¼ cup water, the yeast and sugar, and allow it to stand for 5 minutes.

Add the remaining water and salt.

Gradually blend in 5 cups of the flour, about ½ cup at a time, mixing well after each addition.

Knead until the dough is smooth and stretches, and add enough flour to make a soft dough that does not stick to your hands.

Form a ball from the dough and place it in a buttered bowl, turning so that all sides of the ball are covered with butter.

Cover the bowl with a towel and allow the dough to rise in a warm place such as a turned off oven until it doubles in size, about 1½ hours.

Divide the dough into 4 pieces, and shape each into a ball. Roll each ball out onto a floured board to about ½-inch thickness to form a round 8 inches in diameter.

Brush the rounds with cold water, using a pastry brush.

Cover the rounds with a towel and allow them to stand for 30 minutes.

Preheat the oven to 500 degrees and heat 2 baking sheets in the oven for 10 minutes.

Brush the dough again with cold water.

Press down the center of each round with the heel of your hand to form a circular indentation and prick all over with the tines of a fork to form a design.

Sprinkle with the white and black sesame seeds.

Using potholders, carefully remove the baking sheets from the oven (they will be very hot).

Sprinkle the rounds lightly with more cold water, and place them on the sheets.

Place a few ice cubes on a baking dish on the bottom of the oven to create some steam, and bake on the lowest rack until breads are golden and baked through, about 12–16 minutes.

Makes 4 breads (2–3 servings per bread).

🌿 BUKHARAN FLATBREAD
(Non)

1 envelope dry yeast
2 teaspoons sugar
1 tablespoon salt
2 cups warm water
¼ cup vegetable oil
2½ pounds (8 cups) flour

Combine the yeast, sugar and salt in ½ cup warm water in a large bowl.

Slowly add the oil and the rest of the water, beating until smooth.

Gradually sprinkle in the flour, stirring first with a wooden spoon and then kneading with your hands to form a stiff dough.

Knead until the dough is elastic and no longer sticks to your hands, adding flour as needed.

Place the dough in a lightly buttered bowl and cover with a kitchen towel.

Allow the dough to stand in a warm place such as a turned-off oven for 1½ hours, until it doubles in size.

Divide the dough into 7–8 balls.

Roll out the balls on a floured board to about 12 inches in diameter and ¼ to ⅛-inch thick. Be sure to keep the breads fairly thin.

Prick the dough all over with the tines of a fork.

Place the breads on dry baking sheets.

Preheat the oven to broil.

Bake for 3–5 minutes, watching carefully to be sure the breads do not burn; they should just turn golden brown.

Makes 7–8 breads.

❧ STEAMED CORIANDER BUNS
(Yutangza)

(Adapted from Anya von Bremzen and John Welchman, *Please to the Table*: New York: Workman Publishing, 1990).

1 envelope active dry yeast
2 teaspoons sugar
½ cup lukewarm water (110–115 degrees)
½ cup milk
½ teaspoon salt
3 to 3½ cups all-purpose unbleached flour
8 tablespoons (1 stick) unsalted butter, melted
1 cup finely chopped fresh coriander

In a large bowl mix together the yeast, sugar, and water and set it aside for 5 minutes.

Heat the milk in a small pot until bubbles just form around the edges; the milk should not boil.

Add it together with the salt and 2 tablespoons of flour to the yeast mixture, and beat well with a wooden spoon.

Gradually stir in 3 cups of flour, place the dough on a floured board and, adding flour as needed, knead it until it is smooth and no longer sticks to your hands.

Form the dough into a ball and place it in a buttered bowl and turn it so that all sides are coated with butter.

Cover the ball of dough with a light kitchen towel and let it rise in a warm place such as a turned-off oven, free from drafts for about 1½ hours, until it has doubled in size.

Punch down the dough and knead it for a few minutes.

Divide the dough into 16 parts and form each into a ball.

On a floured board and using a floured rolling pin roll each ball out to form a very thin circle about ⅟₁₆-inch thick.

Brush the dough circle with melted butter and sprinkle with coriander.

Fold the edges of the round to meet in the center and roll the dough smooth between your hands, pinching the ends shut.

Do the same with each ball.

Place the balls on a buttered baking sheet, brush them lightly with more melted butter, cover the sheet with the kitchen towel and allow the buns to rise for 20 more minutes.

Heat water to boiling in the bottom of a large steamer, place the buns in the steamer, lower the heat, partially cover the steamer and steam the buns over the simmering water for about 20 minutes, until the dough is cooked through.

Do not try to steam too many buns at once; they must not touch each other.

Serve warm.

Makes 16 buns.

DESSERTS

Uzbek desserts consist primarily of dried fruits and nuts, baked and fried cookies and fritters, or sweets and candies made from fruit syrups, nuts and honey. Balls of roasted ground walnuts and treats such as *halva* are very popular, as are sweetened stuffed fruit, fruit in syrup, or the fried sugared noodles, *chakchak*. A tray of Uzbek sweets might include almonds, walnuts, pistachios, raisins, dried apricots and walnuts. *Nishalda*, a popular dessert, is a mixture including stiffly beaten egg whites, sugar and licorice; *navot*, a candy that looks like small transparent ice cubes stuck together, is made from white grape juice and sugar, and *kazinaki* closely resembles almond brittle. Some of these desserts have not been included because of the difficulty in obtaining ingredients.

Though Uzbek cuisine does not feature cakes, pies, or puddings, there are excellent recipes for various pastries and cookies. *Paklama* (similar to Greek *baklava*) consists of thin layers of dough with a honey and walnut filling. An assortment of hard cookies made with nuts and jam are served with tea, and the influence of Russian cooking is felt in the cakes which are popular in Tashkent restaurants.

APPLES IN SYRUP
(Sharbatli olma)

4 small apples
1½ cups sugar
2 cups water
½ teaspoon lemon juice
¼ cup white wine

Peel and core the apples.

Heat the sugar and water together, stirring constantly.

When the sugar has melted, add the lemon juice and continue stirring until the mixture is smooth and syrupy.

Carefully lower the apples into the syrup, turning them so that all sides are covered with syrup, and cook on low heat for 15 minutes.

Turn off the heat and remove the apples from the syrup. Add the wine to the syrup and stir well.

Pour the syrup into a bowl, return the apples to the syrup, and chill.

To serve, place each apple on a plate or in a small bowl and pour some of the syrup over it.

Serves 4.

🦁 WALNUT-FILLED QUINCE
(Behbi duilma)

4 medium quinces, peeled and cored
2 teaspoons butter
2 teaspoons honey
⅓ cup raisins
½ cup finely chopped walnuts
2 tablespoons sugar
Vanilla-flavored whipped cream or vanilla ice cream
(optional)

Cut out about 1 inch of fruit from the center of the quinces, leaving a very thick shell.

In the center of each quince, place ½ teaspoon butter and ½ teaspoon honey.

Place the quinces on a steamer (you can use a double boiler) and steam for 40 minutes).

While the quinces are steaming put the raisins in hot water to soften them.

Toast the walnuts for 2 to 3 minutes until they are golden brown and combine them with the raisins and sugar.

The steamed quinces should be about half full with the honey and butter mixture; pour off any extra.

Fill each quince with some of the raisin and nut mixture. The dessert may be topped with vanilla-flavored whipped cream or ice cream.

Serves 4.

🥀 SOUR CREAM POPPY SEED CAKE

(Adapted from *Taste the World with Seattle's Sister Cities*: Kearney, NE: Morris Press, 1989)

½ cup poppy seeds
3 eggs
1½ cups sugar
1½ cups sour cream
1¼ teaspoons vanilla extract
2¼ cups flour
2 teaspoons baking powder
½ teaspoon baking soda
Pinch salt
¼ cup powdered confectioners' sugar

Pour boiling water over the poppy seeds and set them aside for 15 minutes.

Drain well and spread out on a linen towel to dry.

Beat the eggs well, and gradually add the sugar, beating until the mixture is light and fluffy.

Beat in the sour cream and the vanilla extract.

Sift the flour with the baking powder, baking soda, and salt.

Gradually fold the flour into the egg mixture, alternating with the poppy seeds.

Pour the batter into a greased and floured 10-inch bundt pan.

Preheat the oven to 350 degrees. Bake for 50–60 minutes, or until a cake tester comes out clean.

Allow to cool on a rack for 10 minutes, and remove from pan.

Cool completely, and sprinkle with the confectioners' sugar.

Makes 10–12 servings.

🌿 TASHKENT BAKLAVA

(Courtesy of Lydia Barrett, Kaleenka Restaurant, Seattle)

PASTRY
3 cups ground walnuts
½ teaspoon cinnamon
½ teaspoon ground cardamom
½ cup sugar
½ pound phyllo dough sheets, 10 × 12 inches
    (approximately)
½ pound melted sweet butter (approximately)

GLAZE
2 cups water
1 cup honey
1 teaspoon rose water or orange flower water

248

In a bowl blend the walnuts, cinnamon, cardamom and sugar.

Butter a baking sheet and place 1 sheet of the phyllo dough on it; brush with melted butter.

Repeat the process with two more sheets of phyllo dough.

Brush the top layer of phyllo with butter and sprinkle with a thin layer of the nut mixture.

Continue layering the phyllo dough, brushing with butter and sprinkling with a layer of nuts until all the nuts are used up, about 5–6 layers.

Place another sheet of phyllo on the top layer of nuts, brush with butter, and continue with another 2–3 layers of phyllo. Brush the top layer with butter, adding more butter if needed.

Preheat the oven to 300 degrees.

Cut the *baklava* with a sharp knife into diamonds or squares.

Bake at 300 degrees for 1 hour, until top is crisp and pale gold.

Blend the water, honey, and rose or orange flower water, and heat gently for 2–3 minutes on low to medium heat. Do not boil.

Remove the *baklava* and pour the honey glaze over it slowly, allowing the pastry to absorb the liquid. It will remain very moist; do not worry if there is a little extra glaze in the pan.

Allow to cool for 45 minutes. Drain off any extra glaze and serve.

Makes about 24 pieces.

🦂 LAYERED WALNUT PASTRY
(Paklama)

DOUGH
5 eggs
½ cup milk
4 cups flour
¼ teaspoon salt

FILLING
1¾ cups coarsely ground walnut
1½ cups sugar

EGG GLAZE
1 egg yolk
2 teaspoons water

BUTTER AND HONEY SYRUP
6 tablespoons butter, melted
½ cup honey, slightly warmed

Beat the eggs well and blend in the milk.

Combine the flour and salt and gradually stir into the egg mixture until the dough begins to form.

Knead it until the dough is stiff and no longer sticks to your hands.

Set the dough aside for 30 minutes in a bowl covered by a damp kitchen towel.

Toast the ground walnuts for 2–3 minutes in a toaster oven or under the broiler, taking care to see they do not burn.

Combine them with the sugar.

On a floured board form the dough into a long (about 16 inches) "sausage," and divide it into 8 parts.

Form each of them into a ball and allow them to rest for 5 minutes.

Roll each disk out into a circle approximately 8 inches in diameter and about ⅛ to ¹⁄₁₆-inch thick.

Place the first circle on a greased cookie sheet. Sprinkle some of the walnut mixture over the dough circle, cover with the second circle, sprinkle it with more of the walnut mixture, and continue alternating dough circles and walnut filling until the last circle is on top.

Pat down the edges so that the *paklama* forms a smooth round circle.

Beat the egg yolk with the 2 teaspoons water and brush it over the top of the dough.

Make deep cuts from the center to the edge of the circle, dividing the cake into wedges, and then make cuts forming a concentric circle around the cake approximately through the middle.

Preheat the oven to 350 degrees.

Pour the melted butter *slowly* over the cake, giving it time to seep into the cuts and penetrate the dough and filling.

Do not worry if the butter spills out onto the baking sheet.

Bake for 10 minutes.

Remove from the oven and slowly pour the slightly heated honey over the cake so that it also penetrates the dough and filling.

Return the *paklama* to the oven and bake for another 30–40 minutes until golden brown, basting once or twice with any extra butter or honey that may be at the bottom of the pan.

Remove from the oven and allow to cool *completely* before cutting the *paklama* with a very sharp knife.

Serves 8–10.

🐝 BUKHARAN TEA PASTRY
(Leikakh)

¾ cup vegetable oil such as corn oil (do not use olive oil)
1 envelope dry yeast
¼ cup warm water
4 eggs
½ cup sugar
½ teaspoon vanilla
¼ cup vodka
4 to 4½ cups flour

⅔ cup coarsely chopped walnuts
1 egg yolk
1 teaspoon water
½ cup sugar

Heat the oil until warm but not hot.

In a large bowl dissolve the yeast in the warm water and then pour in the oil, stirring constantly.

Beat in the eggs one by one, and then blend in the sugar, vanilla, and vodka.

Gradually sprinkle in the flour, beating with a wooden spoon until the mixture is stiff enough to knead with your hands.

Add just enough flour to form a malleable dough.

Work the dough for 5 minutes until it no longer sticks to your palms. Form into a ball, place into a bowl, cover the bowl with a wet dish towel and place it in a warm place to rise for 1½–2 hours (a turned-off oven is fine).

Preheat the oven to 425 degrees.

Divide the dough into 6 parts.

Turn out each section of the dough onto a floured board and roll with a floured rolling pin to form a rectangle or diamond approximately 6 × 4 inches in size, and about ½-inch thick.

Sprinkle a tablespoon or so of the nuts into the center of each rectangle. Blend the egg yolk with the water, and brush it around the sides of the dough not covered by the nuts.

Sprinkle the entire pastry with sugar.

Place the 6 pastries on a lightly greased baking sheet and bake for 18–25 minutes, until pastries are golden brown.

Cool thoroughly before serving.

Makes 6 pastries, each about 4–5 servings.

These are excellent served with tea and jam.

⚜ FRIED WALNUT SAMSAS
(Entok samsa)

DOUGH
1½ cups all-purpose flour
Pinch salt
4 tablespoons (½ stick) softened butter
⅔ cup lukewarm water (105–115 degrees)

FILLING
7 ounces walnuts, ground (this can be done in a food
    processor)
1½ tablespoons softened butter
1½ tablespoons sugar

Vegetable oil for frying (about 4 cups)
Confectioners' sugar

Place the flour in a large bowl and make a well in the center.

Sprinkle the salt into the well, add 2 tablespoons of the butter and pour in the water, stirring until the ingredients are well blended.

Beat the mixture with a wooden spoon and then knead it with your hands until it forms a ball.

Roll out the ball of dough on a floured surface into a large rectangle, about 15 by 17 inches.

Brush the dough with the remaining softened butter, fold it into quarters, and roll it out again.

Cut the resulting rectangle into 2-inch squares.

Mix the ground walnuts, 1½ tablespoons softened butter and the sugar together until well blended.

Place 1 teaspoon of this filling on each square of dough, and draw up the corners in the middle.

Dip your fingers in water and pinch the ends together tightly.

Fill a deep, heavy pot with 4 inches of oil and heat until it is very hot, about 375 degrees on a deep-fat thermometer.

Drop in 8 or 9 of the *samsas*, turning them occasionally with a slotted spoon, and cook for about 3–4 minutes, until they are crisp and golden brown.

Remove with a slotted spoon and drain well on paper towels.

Sprinkle lightly with confectioners' sugar.

Makes about 20 samsas.

❦ FRIED SWEET COOKIES
(Urama)

2 eggs
½ cup granulated sugar
½ cup milk
½ cup (5 tablespoons) butter, melted
1 teaspoon cognac
¼ teaspoon salt
3⅓ cups flour (approximately
1½ cups vegetable oil such as corn oil (approximately)
Confectioners' sugar

Beat the eggs well and add the sugar, beating until mixture is well blended.

Stir in the milk, butter, cognac and salt, and then gradually sprinkle in the flour until the mixture forms a stiff dough.

Roll it out to ¼-inch thickness and, using a pizza or pastry cutter, cut out strips 1 inch wide and about 6 inches long.

Roll up strip lightly, pinching one end to form a small, loosely fastened roll.

Heat the oil in a frying pan until it is very hot, and drop in the rolled strips.

Fry quickly until golden brown, turning once carefully with tongs; take care to keep the oil from spattering.

Do not overcrowd the pastries, or they will not brown properly.

Remove with tongs and allow them to dry on paper towels.

When cool sprinkle generously with confectioners' sugar.

Makes about 2 dozen.

These are very good with tea and jam.

🦁 *LAKOMKA* JAM COOKIES

1½ sticks (12 tablespoons) sweet butter, softened
1 cup sugar
2 eggs
1 teaspoon vanilla extract
1¾ cups flour

½ cup jam (blackberry, strawberry, raspberry or cherry)

Cream the butter with the sugar until white and then beat in the eggs one by one.

Stir in the vanilla and gradually sprinkle in the flour, beating until smooth. The dough will be soft.

Drop by teaspoonfuls onto a greased baking sheet, leaving plenty of space between the cookies, as they will spread.

Bake for 10–15 minutes in a 350-degree oven until golden brown around the edges.

Allow the cookies to cool for 5 minutes before removing from sheet.

With a spatula spread a little jam on the bottom of one cookie and press it to the bottom of a second cookie.

Allow them to cool at room temperature.

Makes 18 jam-filled cookies or 3 dozen without the jam.

Note: You can also make the cookies without the jam filling, though it adds a lot to them!

🦌 *NARGIZ* MERINGUE COOKIES

3 egg whites
Pinch salt
½ cup sugar
½ teaspoon vanilla
3 tablespoons (approximately) poppy seeds
⅔ cup raspberry jam (optional)

Have the egg whites at room temperature.

Beat them until soft peaks form and gradually sprinkle in the salt and sugar, beating until the mixture stands in stiff peaks.

Beat in the vanilla and stir in the poppy seeds.

Preheat oven to 225 degrees.

Line a baking sheet with foil.

Pipe the meringue through a pastry bag onto the sheet to form strips about 2 inches long and ¾-inch wide.

Bake for about 30–40 minutes until set and very lightly browned. (Baking time may vary depending on the thickness of the strips and the heat of the oven. Start checking after 30 minutes).

Cool the meringues on the baking sheet on a rack for 15 minutes.

Carefully remove them with a spatula.

If you are using the jam, spread it with a small spatula on the underside of a meringue, and join it to another meringue.

Cool completely before serving.

Makes about 30 strips or 15 jam meringues.

❧ WALNUT MERINGUES

(Adapted from *Taste the World with Seattle's Sister Cities*: Kearney, NE: Morris Press, 1989)

4 egg whites
1½ cups sugar
1 tablespoon lemon juice
2 cups finely chopped (but not grated) walnuts

Combine the egg whites, sugar and lemon juice in the top of a double boiler. Heat the boiler on medium-low heat.

Beat with an electric mixer at medium high speed for about 6–8 minutes, until the mixture stands in glossy stiff peaks.

Remove from heat and stir in the nuts.

Drop by teaspoonfuls on a well greased cookie sheet to form small mounds. Do not flatten.

Preheat the oven to 300 degrees, and bake for 10–25 minutes, until meringues are set and just starting to turn golden brown.

Remove carefully from baking sheet, using a large spatula, as the cookies are fragile. Allow to cool.

Makes 5 dozen meringues.

❧ ORIENTAL COOKIES
(Vostochnoe)

14 tablespoons (1¼ sticks) butter, at room temperature
1 cup sugar
3 eggs, separated
½ teaspoon vanilla
3 cups flour
½ teaspoon baking soda
⅔ cup raisins
⅔ cup coarsely crushed walnuts

Cream the butter with the sugar, and beat in the egg yolks one at a time.

Stir in the vanilla.

Combine the flour and baking soda and sprinkle it into the dough, stirring, and then knead to form a fairly stiff dough.

Wet your hands and form the dough into balls approximately 1½ inches in diameter.

Make an indentation in the center of each ball, place 2–3 raisins in the dough, close the ball and flatten it.

Beat the egg whites slightly, and either dip the cookie into the egg whites or brush it lightly with them.

Sprinkle the top of the cookie with the crushed nuts and pat them down to keep the nuts from falling off.

Preheat the oven to 350 degrees.

Bake the cookies on a buttered and floured baking sheet for 15–20 minutes until they are lightly browned and firm to the touch.

Cool for 20 minutes on the baking sheet on a rack before removing them.

Makes about 3 dozen cookies.

🦁 FRIED SWEET NOODLES
(Chakchak)

3¾ cups flour
Pinch salt
½ teaspoon baking soda
¼ teaspoon white vinegar
7 eggs, well beaten
1 tablespoon cognac
1 cup vegetable oil
2½ cups honey
1½ cups sugar
1 tablespoon butter

Blend the flour and salt in a large bowl.

Dissolve the baking soda in the vinegar and add to the flour.

Make a well in the center and stir in the eggs and cognac, and knead to form a dough that sticks together.

Form the dough into a ball, roll it in a damp kitchen towel and set it aside in a bowl for 20 minutes.

Roll out the dough on a floured board to ½-inch thickness, and cut into small strips ¼-inch wide and ½-inch long.

Heat the oil until it is very hot and carefully fry the dough strips in batches, stirring, until they are golden brown, about 4 minutes.

With a slotted spoon or spatula remove them to paper towels to drain. Add more oil if needed, and take care that the oil does not spatter.

Heat the honey and sugar in a pot over medium heat, stirring until the sugar is completely dissolved and the mixture is thick.

Place the dough strips in a large bowl and carefully pour the honey mixture over them.

Stir gently to coat all the strips, taking care not to mash them.

Turn the strips out on to a large, well-buttered plate, mounding the mixture in the center.

Cover the mound with plastic wrap, pressing it on all sides so that the pieces of dough stick to each other. Allow the *chakchak* to stand for 1 hour.

Use a sharp knife to cut off servings of the *chakchak*.

Serves 10.

This pastry is good with tea or coffee. It can also be served with a scoop of vanilla ice cream on top of some *chakchak*, or with a slice of honeydew melon.

 HALVA

1 pound white sesame seeds
Pinch cinnamon
⅛ teaspoon powdered nutmeg
⅛ teaspoon powdered cloves
⅛ teaspoon powdered cardamom
2 cups sugar
⅓ cup water

Place the sesame seeds, cinnamon, nutmeg, cloves and cardamom in a food processor and pulse until the ingredients stick together.

Heat the sugar and water over medium heat, stirring constantly, and simmer on low heat for 10–12 minutes, until the syrup thickens.

Add the syrup to the sesame seed paste and continue to pulse gently until the mixture is smooth.

Place the halva in a shallow dish and smooth the top.

When the mixture has cooled cut it into 1-inch cubes.

Makes about 1½ pounds halva.

❧ ALMONDS IN SUGAR

2¼ cups sugar
⅔ cup water
8 ounces almonds, blanched
1 tablespoon softened butter

In a heavy pot combine 1 cup of the sugar and the water, and bring to a boil.

Add the almonds and cook over low to medium heat, stirring constantly, for about 10–12 minutes.

Add the remaining cup of sugar and continue to cook, stirring, for another 3–4 minutes.

The mixture will become very thick.

Carefully pour the hot nut-sugar blend into a bowl and melt the remaining ¼ cup sugar in the heavy pot, stirring as it begins to caramelize.

Quickly return the nuts to the pot and stir vigorously until the nuts and sugar begin to turn dark brown.

Keep stirring to prevent them from burning.

Remove from heat, blend in the butter, and quickly turn the almonds out onto a well-buttered plate, pressing them with a spatula to form a single layer.

Allow the nuts to cool until they can be handled.

Separate any which may be sticking together, breaking off extra pieces of sugar which may have stuck to them.

Do not wait until the mixture has cooled completely, as this will produce a rock-hard candy.

Makes about 2 cups.

The nuts are good with tea and dried fruit.

🌿 LEMON JAM

5 lemons, cut in eighths and seeded, but with rind
2 oranges, cut in eighths and seeded, but with rind
Water
2 cups sugar (approximately)

Soak the lemon and orange pieces in about 10 cups water for 24 hours.

Bring the fruit pieces to a boil in the same water in which they were soaked.

Simmer for 1½ hours in a heavy pot on very low heat, adding water as necessary to keep the jam from burning.

Add the sugar gradually, stirring constantly and tasting.

Continue to add sugar until desired sweetness and thickness is obtained.

Cook for 30 more minutes on very low heat.

Cool thoroughly before serving.

Makes 2–3 cups jam.

Serve with tea and cookies.

🥕 CARROT JAM

1 pound carrots, peeled
Water
2 cups sugar
Peel of 1 lemon, coarsely chopped

Juice of 1 lemon

Cut the carrots into ½-inch thick slices.

Boil the carrots in water to cover until tender.

Drain well and sprinkle them with ½ cup sugar.

Cook the lemon peel in boiling water to cover for 1 minute.

Drain the lemon peel well and add it to the carrots.

Add ⅔ cup water to the carrots and cook in a heavy pot over very low heat, stirring.

Add water as necessary to keep the carrots from burning.

Taste for seasoning, and add remaining sugar and lemon juice to taste.

Simmer until a thick syrup forms and the carrots are almost transparent, at least 30 minutes.

Makes about 3 cups jam.

Serve with tea and cookies.

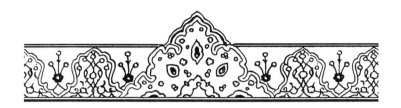

DRINKS

Several varieties of green tea and black tea are available in Uzbekistan, and these are always served unsweetened. The cups are never filled to the brim, for that would be a sign that a guest is expected to drink up and leave; the half-empty cup is a sign that more is coming. Tea is usually served with sweets or cookies, or with various preserves spooned into little round glass dishes. Tea with honey, milk, salt or butter, and fruit teas are served more rarely. Though the sweetened fruit drinks made from slowly simmering fresh or dried fruit with water and sugar are called *kompot*, these Uzbek preparations should not be confused with American compotes, for they contain mostly liquid and only a few pieces of fruit.

❧ TEA WITH BLACK PEPPER AND HONEY
(Assali murch choi)

1 teaspoon black tea
2 teaspoons honey
Pinch fresh, finely ground black pepper
2 cups boiling water

Place the tea, honey and pepper in a teapot and pour in the boiling water.

Allow the tea to steep for 4–5 minutes.

Stir well, strain, and serve.

Makes 2 cups tea.

You can vary the amount of tea depending on how strong you like the brew. This is often served as a remedy for colds.

🌿 TEA WITH MILK AND BUTTER
(Chau khi moi)

1 cup water
1 heaping tablespoon green tea
2 cups milk (do not use skim milk)
1½ teaspoons butter
1 small Uzbek *non* bread or pita bread, torn into
    small pieces

In a pot bring the water to a boil and add the tea.

Simmer on very low heat for 5 minutes, and add the milk.

Bring to a boil, reduce the heat, and simmer for another 5 minutes.

Remove from heat and strain into cups.

Stir ½ teaspoon butter into each cup.

Break the bread into very small pieces and dip them into the tea while drinking the tea.

Makes 3 small cups tea.

Note: You can omit the butter, as this is a bit of an acquired taste!

❧ COLD SPICED HONEY TEA
(Dolchinli asal choi)

3 teaspoons honey
4 cups hot black tea
½ teaspoon cinnamon

Stir the honey into the hot tea and add the cinnamon.

Pour the mixture into a heat-proof pitcher and chill.

Serves 4.

❧ ICED APPLE TEA
(Mevali choi)

2 teaspoons sugar
2 cups hot strong black tea
⅔ cup apple juice
3 thin slices lemon

Dissolve the sugar in the hot tea.

Add the apple juice and lemon slices, pour into a pitcher and cool.

Serve over ice cubes.

Makes 2–3 drinks.

🌺 DRIED APRICOT DRINK
(Bargak ichimligi)

¾ pound dried apricots
8 cups water

Rinse the apricots in a sieve and place in a bowl.

Bring the water to a boil and pour over the apricots.

Cover and allow the mixture to steep for 24 hours.

Place two or three pieces of dried apricot in the bottom of each glass and add the apricot liquid.

Serve at room temperature.

Serves 8.

🦁 WATERMELON DRINK
(Tarvuz kompoti)

8 cups water
1½ cups sugar
2 cups watermelon, seeded and cut into 1-inch cubes

Bring the water and sugar to a boil, stirring to melt the sugar.

Lower the heat and simmer for 5 minutes.

Add the watermelon pieces and return to a boil.

Lower the heat and simmer for another 5 minutes.

Cool thoroughly and pour into glasses, being sure there are a few pieces of watermelon in each glass.

Serves 6.

❧ YOGURT DRINK
(Airan)

2 containers (8 ounces each) low-fat unflavored yogurt
1 cup unflavored seltzer water
⅛ teaspoon salt

Combine all three ingredients and chill well.

Serve with two or three small pieces of ice in each glass.

Makes 2–4 small drinks.

A FEW
SUGGESTED MENUS

Cold Sour Milk and Herbs Soup, p. 88
Guliston Chicken Salad, p. 46
Onion Flatbread, p. 236
Ice Cream and Tashkent *Baklava*, p. 248

Cucumber and Radish Salad, p. 27
Lamb *Plov Kovurma*, p. 143
Tomato and Cucumber Salad, p. 25
Walnut Meringues, p. 258
Almonds in Sugar, p. 262

Fish Salad, p. 48
Steamed Lamb Dumplings, p. 165
White Radish and Pomegranate Salad, p. 30
Lakomka Jam Cookies, p. 256
Vanilla Ice Cream

White Cheese Salad, p. 42
Liver *Shashlyk*, p. 120
Scallion Pancakes, p. 208
White Radish and Almond Salad, p. 31
Fried Walnut *Samsas*, p. 253

Tashkent Beef and Cabbage Soup, p. 61
Bukharan Flatbread, p. 239
Steamed Fish, p. 132
Fried Mushrooms, p. 221
Oriental Cookies, p. 259
Tea

Lagman Meat, Noodle and Vegetable Stew, p. 197
Fish Cutlets *Po-Munaiski*, p. 136
Radish and Egg Salad, p. 28
Apples in Syrup, p. 245

Chicken and Spinach Soup, p. 77
Baked Lamb Stew Samarkand, p. 100
Spring Salad, p. 26
Walnut-Filled Quinces, p. 246
Tea

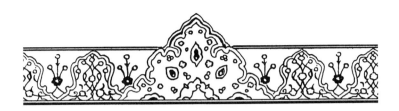

INDEX

Also by Lynn Visson

WEDDED STRANGERS: The Challenges of Russian-American Marriages

In this fascinating study of the issues that Russian-American couples must confront, Dr. Lynn Visson explores such questions as: Why are Americans and Russians so intensely attracted to each other? What do they expect from romance and marriage? For better or worse, how do they live together? Why do these couples have such frequent misunderstandings when they are fluent in each other's language? With numerous examples and case studies garnered from ten years of research and interviews with nearly 100 couples, the author provides significant and often startling insights into the unique challenges and problems facing Russian-American couples.

243 pages • 5½ x 8½ • 0-7818-0646-1 • W • $24.95hc • (728)

Other Cookbooks of Interest from HIPPOCRENE

THE BEST OF RUSSIAN COOKING, Expanded Edition
Alexandra Kropotkin

"Russia has a decided culinary heritage. This book reflects that heritage better than any volume I know." —Craig Claiborne

Updated with complete list of menu terms, this comprehensive Russian cookbook includes 300 easy-to-follow recipes for traditional favorites.

288 pages • 5½ x 8½ • 0-7818-0131-1 • $11.95pb • (251)

THE BEST OF UKRAINIAN CUISINE, Expanded Edition
Bohdan Zahny

Now updated with a complete list of menu terms in Ukrainian and English, this unique cookbook presents both traditional and contemporary Ukrainian cuisine in an easy-to-use menu format.

300 pages • 5½ x 8½ • 0-7818-0654-2 • $12.95pb • (738)

EGYPTIAN COOKING
Samia Abdennour

Nearly 400 recipes, all adapted for the North American kitchen, represent the best of authentic Egyptian family cooking

199 pages • 5½ x8½ • 0-7818-0643-7 • $11.95pb • (727)

THE ART OF PERSIAN COOKING
Forough Hekmat

This collection of 200 recipes features such traditional Persian dishes as Abgushte Adas (Lentil Soup), Mosamme Khoreshe (Eggplant Stew), Lamb Kebab, Cucumber Borani (Special Cucumber Salad), Sugar Halva and Gol Moraba (Flower Preserves).

190 pages • 5½ x 8½ • 0-7818-0241-5 • $9.95pb • (125)

THE ART OF ISRAELI COOKING
Chef Aldo Nahoum

"[Includes] a host of new indigenous Israeli recipes with dishes that reflect the eclectic and colorful nature of Israeli cuisine." —*Jewish Week*

125 pages • 5½ x 8½ • 0-7818-0096-X • $9.95pb • (252)

THE ART OF TURKISH COOKING
Nesret Eren

"Her recipes are utterly mouthwatering, and I cannot remember a time when a book so inspired me to take pot in hand."

—Nika Hazelton, *The New York Times Book Review*

308 pages • 5½ x 8½ • 0-7818-0201-6 • W • $12.95pb • (162)

THE JOY OF CHINESE COOKING
Doreen Yen Hung Feng

Includes over 200 kitchen-tested recipes and a thorough index.

226 pages • 5½ x 7½ • illustrations • 0-7818-0097-8 • $8.95pb • (288)

ART OF SOUTH INDIAN COOKING
Alamelu Vairavan and Patricia Marquardt

Over 100 recipes for tempting appetizers, chutneys, rice dishes, vegetables and stews—flavored with onions, tomatoes, garlic, and delicate spices in varying combinations—have been adapted for the Western kitchen.

202 pages • 5½ x 8½ • 0-7818-0525-2 • W • $22.50 • (635)

BEST OF GOAN COOKING
Gilda Mendonsa

This book is a rare and authentic collection of over 130 of the finest Goan recipes and 12 pages of full color illustrations. From Goa—a region in Western India once colonized by the Portuguese—comes a cuisine in which the hot, sour and spicy flavors mingle in delicate perfection, a reflection of the combination of Arabian, Portuguese and Indian cultures that have inhabited the region.

106 pages • 7 x 9¼ • 12 pages color illustrations • 0-7818-0584-8 • NA • $8.95pb • (682)

THE BEST OF KASHMIRI COOKING
Neerja Mattoo
    With nearly 90 recipes and 12 pages of color photographs, this cookbook is a wonderful introduction to Kashmiri dishes, considered the height of gourmet Indian cuisine.
131 pages • 5½ x 8½ • 12 pages color photographs • 0-7818-0612-7 • NA • $9.95pb • (724)

ALL ALONG THE DANUBE:
    Recipes from Germany, Austria, Czechoslovakia, Yugoslavia, Hungary, Romania, and Bulgaria
Marina Polvay
    For novices and gourmets, this unique cookbook offers a tempting variety of over 300 Central European recipes from the shores of the Danube River, bringing Old World flavor to today's dishes.
349 pages • 5½ x 8½ • numerous b/w photos & illustrations • 0-7818-0098-6 • W • $14.95pb • (491)

TASTE OF ROMANIA
Nicolae Klepper
    "A brilliant cultural and culinary history . . . a collection of recipes to be treasured, tested and enjoyed."
            —George Lang, owner of Café des Artistes

    " . . . dishes like creamy cauliflower soup, sour cream-enriched *mamaliga* (the Romanian polenta), lamb stewed in sauerkraut juice and scallions, and *mititei* (exactly like the ones I tasted so long ago in Bucharest) are simple and appealing . . . Klepper paints a pretty picture of his native country's culinary possibilities."   —Colman Andrews, *Saveur* magazine
    A real taste of both Old World and modern Romanian culture. More than 140 recipes, including the specialty dishes of Romania's top chefs, are inter-mingled with fables, poetry, photos and illustrations in this comprehensive and well-organized guide to Romanian cuisine.
319 pages • 5½ x 8½ • photos/illustrations • 0-7818-0523-6 • W • $24.95hc • (637)

TRADITIONAL BULGARIAN COOKING
Atanas Slavov
    This collection of over 125 authentic recipes, the first comprehensive Bulgarian cookbook published in English, spans the range of home cooking: including many stews and hearty soups using lamb or poultry and grilled meats, vegetables and cheese pastries; desserts of sweetmeats rich in sugar and honey, puddings, and dried fruit compotes.
200 pages • 5½ x 8½ • 0-7818-0581-3 • W • $22.50hc • (681)

THE BEST OF CZECH COOKING

Peter Trnka

Over 200 simple yet elegant recipes from this little-known cuisine.

248 pages • 5 x 8½ • 0-7818-0492-2 • W • $12.95pb • (376)

ART OF LITHUANIAN COOKING

Maria Gieysztor de Gorgey

With over 150 recipes, this cookbook is a collection of traditional hearty Lithuanian favorites like Fresh Cucumber Soup, Lithuanian Meat Pockets, Hunter's Stew, Potato Zeppelins, and delicacies like Homemade Honey Liqueur and Easter Gypsy Cake.

176 pages • 5½ x 8½ • 0-7818-0610-0 • W • $24.95hc • (722)

BEST OF ALBANIAN COOKING: FAVORITE FAMILY RECIPES

Klementina and R. John Hysa

Over 100 recipes cover every aspect of the Albanian meal, with sections on inviting meze-s (appetizers) and turshi-s (pickles) through Meat, Poultry and Rabbit, Vegetables, Soups, Fish, Pasta and Pies, Sauces, Compotes and Desserts, and Drinks.

176 pages • 5½ x 8½ • 0-7818-0609-7 • $22.50hc • (721)

THE ART OF HUNGARIAN COOKING, Revised edition

Paul Pogany Bennett and Velma R. Clark

Whether you crave Chicken Paprika or Apple Strudel, these 222 authentic Hungarian recipes inlude a vast array of national favorites, from appetizers through desserts. Now updated with a concise guide to Hungarian wines!

225 pages • 5½ x 8½ • 18 b/w drawings • 0-7818-0586-4 • W • $11.95pb • (686)

All prices subject to change. **To purchase Hippocrene Books** contact your local bookstore, call (718) 454-2366, or write to: HIPPOCRENE BOOKS, 171 Madison Avenue, New York, NY 10016. Please enclose check or money order, adding $5.00 shipping (UPS) for the first book and $.50 for each additional book.